THE BEST OF NEWSPAPER DESIGN

14th edition

The Society of Newspaper Design's
Annual Awards Competition

The Society of Newspaper Design
The Newspaper Center
Box 4075
Reston, VA 22090

ROCKPORT
PUBLISHERS

FIRST PUBLISHED IN THE U.S.A. BY ROCKPORT PUBLISHERS, INC.

CONTENTS

The Society of Newspaper Design
The Newspaper Center
Box 4075
Reston, VA 22090
(703) 620-1083

First published in the United States of America by:
Rockport Publishers, Inc.
146 Granite Street
Rockport, MA 01966
Telephone: (508) 546-9590
Fax: (508) 546-7141
Telex: 5106019284 ROCKORT PUB

Distributed to the book trade and art trade in the U.S. and Canada by:
North Light, an imprint of F & W Publications
1507 Dana Avenue
Cincinnati, OH 45207
Telephone: (513) 531-2222

Other Distribution by:
Rockport Publishers, Inc.
Rockport, MA 01966

ISBN 1-56496-062-5 (Hardcover edition)
ISBN 1-878107-03-8 (Softcover edition)

10 9 8 7 6 5 4 3 2 1

Printed in Singapore by Regent Publishing

Book Credits

DESIGNER & EDITOR
C. Marshall Matlock
*The S.I. Newhouse School
of Public Communications
Syracuse University*

ASSOCIATE EDITOR
Barbara Hines
Howard University

PRODUCTION ASSISTANT
Shamus Walker
Syracuse

COVER CONCEPT
Karen D. Davis
The Dallas Morning News

COVER PHOTO
Leslie White
The Dallas Morning News

SND Officers

President
Nancy Tobin
Tobin Paperworks

1st Vice President
George Benge
News-Leader

2nd Vice President
Deborah Withey
Detroit Free Press

Treasurer
Jim Jennings
Lexington Herald-Leader

Secretary
Neal Pattison
Albuquerque Tribune

Immediate Past President
Randy Stano
The Miami Herald

SND Executive Director
Ray Chattman

Introduction

For three very cold days in early February 1993, 16 judges from the United States and Spain spent more than 32 hours poring over 8,200-plus entries in the Society of Newspaper Design's 14th Edition international design competition.

As the judging at Syracuse University progressed, one point became clear – *The Miami Herald* set a new standard in journalism with its coverage of Hurricane Andrew. That opinion was strong and unanimous – so strong that *The Herald* received the only Best of Show awarded in the competition. Best of Show, the highest level of award in the contest, must be agreed on by the entire judging team.

Judges were impressed with *The Herald's* work on several levels. It was comprehensive; it was insightful; it explained for the newspaper's readers what had happened to them and their neighbors; it told them what to do day by day. *The Herald* became not only a communication medium for the residents of the devastated areas, it also became a voice to the rest of the nation. And, it did these things on a daily basis for weeks after the storm.

But what made this body of work especially significant for the contest judges was the way in which design was the tie that bound the package from concept to execution. While acknowledging that not every element was perfect, judges said the graphics and design of the work obviously were as important as any other element – the reporting, the writing, the editing, the photography. One judge said this effort by *The Herald* could be looked on as a watershed for the Society as well because it exemplified the role design should play as the building block of journalistic planning and execution.

To give you a better idea of what the judges saw, a special section of this annual has been devoted to *The Miami Herald's* coverage of Hurricane Andrew. When you look at these pages, remember the judges recognized the work not only for its design, but also for the extraordinary newsroom teamwork required to produce it.

But many other newspapers – 133 to be exact – also were recognized for their excellent work. When the smoke cleared, judges had awarded 17 Gold awards, 85 Silver awards, 114 Bronze awards, 577 awards of excellence and three Judges' Special Recognition awards in addition to *The Herald's* Best of Show – slightly fewer than the total awarded in the 13th Edition, though more awards were medals.

Judging, as it has been the past four years, was at the S. I. Newhouse School of Public Communications in Syracuse, NY. (Did I mention it was cold – like minus 17 degrees?) This competition would not exist without the efforts – before, during and after the judging – of Marshall Matlock and the 25-plus students from the Newhouse School who provide all of us who fly in for the weekend with everything you could possibly imagine to ensure the contest runs without a hitch. For all of their help, my deepest thanks and appreciation.

Thanks also to Jim Jennings, Randy Stano, Kelly Frankeny, Mike Jantze, Scott Goldman and Jef Capaldi, who helped coordinate judging teams; Barbara Hines, of Howard University, and Ray Chattman, SND's executive director, for managing the database of award winners; Karen Davis, et al, in *The Dallas Morning News* art department for the artwork on the call for entries and the cover of this annual; and my bosses and co-workers at the *Austin American-Statesman,* for understanding when my real job got pushed aside so I could handle my contest duties.

G.W. Babb
14th Edition Chair

Introducción

Durante tres días muy fríos de principios de Febrero de 1993, 16 jueces de los Estados Unidos y de España pasaron más de 32 horas examinando las más de 8200 muestras del concurso internacional de diseño de la 14ava Edición de la Sociedad de Diseño de Periódicos.

Mientras la selección avanzaba en Syracuse University, un punto quedó claro -El Miami Herald estableció un nuevo estándar en periodismo con su cobertura del Huracán Andrew. Esa opinión fue firme y unánime -tan firme que el Herald recibió el único Premio al Mejor del Concurso otorgado en el concurso. El Premio al Mejor del Concurso, el de más alto nivel otorgado en el concurso, requiere que el equipo de jueces al completo esté de acuerdo con su concesión.

Los jueces quedaron impresionados con el trabajo del Herald a varios niveles. Abarcaba mucha información; era profundo; explicaba a los lectores lo que les había sucedido a ellos y a sus vecinos; les indicaba qué hacer día a día. El Herald se convirtió no sólo en un medio de comunicación para los residentes de las zonas devastadas, sino también en una voz para el resto de la nación. E hizo todo eso diariamente durante semanas después de la tormenta.

Pero lo que hizo que este trabajo fuera especialmente significativo para los jueces fue la manera en que el diseño se constituía en el elemento que "ataba" el conjunto desde el concepto a la ejecución. Reconociendo que no todos los elementos eran perfectos, los jueces expresaron que el aspecto gráfico y el trabajo de diseño obviamente habían sido tan importantes como cualquier otro elemento -información, escritura, redacción o fotografía. Un juez dijo que este esfuerzo del Herald también podría considerarse como modelo de línea para la Sociedad porque ejemplificaba el papel que debería desempeñar el diseño como unidad de construcción en la planificación y ejecución periodísticas.

Para proporcionar una mejor idea de lo que vieron los jueces, se ha dedicado una sección especial de esta publicación anual a la cobertura del Huracán Andrew por parte del Miami Herald. Cuando miren estas páginas, recuerden que los jueces reconocieron el trabajo no sólo por su diseño, sino también por el extraordinario trabajo de equipo en la sala de noticias necesario para producirlo.

Pero también muchos otros periódicos -133 para ser exactos- fueron reconocidos por su excelente trabajo. Cuando todo acabó, los jueces habían otorgado 17 premios de Oro, 85 de Plata, 114 de Bronce, 577 premios a la Excelencia y tres premios de Reconocimiento Especial de los Jueces además del Premio al Mejor del Concurso, otorgado al Herald - algo menos del total otorgado en la 13ava Edición, aunque más premios fueron medallas.

La deliberación tuvo lugar, como ha venido siendo en los últimos cuatro años, en la Escuela de Comunicación Pública S. I. Newhouse, en Syracuse, New York. (¿He mencionado ya que hacía frío -algo así como 27ºC bajo cero?) Este concurso no existiría sin los esfuerzos -antes, durante y después de la deliberación- de Marshall Matlock y sus más de 25 estudiantes de la Escuela Newhouse, que nos proporcionaron a todos los que fuimos ese fin de semana todo lo imaginable para asegurarse de que el concurso se desarrollara sin el más mínimo inconveniente. Por toda su ayuda, mi más profundo agradecimiento y aprecio.

Gracias también a Jim Jennings, Randy Stano, Kelly Frankeny, Mike Jantze, Scott Goldman y Jef Capaldi, que ayudaron a coordinar los equipos de jueces; a Barbara Hines, de Howard University, y a Ray Chattman, director ejecutivo de SND, por manejar la base de datos de los ganadores de premios; a Karen Davis y todos los del departamento de arte del Dallas Morning News por el trabajo artístico para la convocatoria y la cubierta de esta publicación anual; y a mis jefes y colegas del Austin American-Statesman, por haber sido comprensivos cuando mi verdadero trabajo tuvo que ser dejado de lado para que yo pudiera ocuparme de mis tareas para el concurso.

G.W. Babb
Presidente de la 14ava Edición

FOREWORD

More than 8,200 entries representing thousands of tear sheets were judged in preparation for the making of this book. Included in the following pages are examples of winning entries. Although it was not possible to include every winning entry, special effort was made to include as many as possible. Slides of all the winning entries are available from the SND's student chapter at the S.I. Newhouse School of Public Communications, Syracuse University.

The judging task started in the spring of 1992 with discussions as to the people who could best represent the Society at the 14th Edition judging. G.W. Babb, 14th Edition chair, worked with the Society's Competition Committee in making the final selection of the 16 judges needed to accomplish the mammoth judging job in just three long days.

The S.I. Newhouse School of Public Communications again cosponsored the judging. Hundreds of tables were set up using a system which allows judges to vote on each entry in the 22 categories and still remain alert after a 10-to-14-hour day.

In case of a conflict, a "floating" judge was asked to judge the entry. A number of qualified "floating" judges were available on the judging floor to perform this duty. A conflict occurs when a judge comes across an entry from his or her publication, a publication he or she has done recent consulting work for (recent is defined as an 18-month period immediately prior to judging) or a publication with which he or she directly competes.

The Society presents four levels of awards:

Award of Excellence is granted for work that is truly excellent. Mere technical or aesthetic competency should not be recognized. But to receive an award these entries need not be "perfect." It is appropriate to honor entries for such things as being daring and innovative if the entry is outstanding but less than 100 percent in every respect.

Bronze Medal is granted for work that stands above the Award of Excellence. It may be granted to any entry receiving three votes in medal discussion by the judging team. The technical proficiency of the Bronze Medal should reach the limits of the medium.

Silver Medal is granted for work that goes beyond excellence. The technical proficiency of the Silver Medal should stretch the limits of the medium. These entries should shine.

Gold Medal is granted for work that defines the state of the art. Such an entry should stretch the limits of creativity. It should be impossible to find anything deficient in a gold-winning entry.

In addition to the Award of Excellence and the three medals, two special honors are possible: the Judges' Special Recognition and the Best of Show. These honors are rare and given only when specific, special circumstances warrant the award.

Judges' Special Recognition: This honor can be awarded by a team of judges or by all judges for work that is outstanding in a particular respect not singled out in the Award of Excellence, Bronze, Silver, or Gold medal structure. This recognition has been granted for such things as use of photography, use of informational graphics and the use of typography throughout a body of work. This body of work may be a particular publication, section or sections by an individual or staff. The special recognition does not supplant any Award of Excellence, Bronze, Silver or Gold and should be seen as an adjunct. In the hierarchy of awards, it falls between the level of the Silver Medal and Gold Medal. It is clearly a step above the Silver Medal because it is normally for a body of work or for consistent excellence, but it does not earn a Gold Medal because of its narrow focus.

Best of Show: As the name implies this is the best of the Gold Medal winners. Any discussion for this award takes place at the conclusion of the judging. Judges had an opportunity to view all Silver and Gold winners at the same time. There is no limit as to the number of Best of Show awards that may be presented in one or more categories. This year one Best of Show was awarded to *The Miami Herald* for its Hurricane Andrew coverage.

DELANTERO

En la preparación de este libro se juzgaron más de 8200 contribuciones representando miles de trabajos publicados. En las páginas siguientes se incluyen ejemplos de los concursantes ganadores. Aunque no fue posible incluir a todos los ganadores, se hizo un esfuerzo especial por incluir el máximo número posible. La división de estudiantes de SND de la Escuela de Comunicaciones Públicas S.I. Newhouse de la Universidad de Syracuse dispone de diapositivas de todas las obras de los concursantes.

La tarea de los jueces comenzó en la primavera de 1992 con discusiones sobre quién representaría mejor a la Sociedad juzgando la 14ava Edición. G.W. Babb, presidente de la 14ava Edición, trabajó con el Comité de Concurso de la Sociedad para hacer la selección final de los 16 jueces necesarios para llevar a término la difícil tarea de juzgar en sólo tres largos días. Una vez más, la Escuela de Comunicaciones Públicas S.I. Newhouse co-patrocinó el juicio. Se instalaron cientos de mesas, utilizando un sistema que permite a los jueces emitir su voto por cada trabajo de las 22 categorías y conseguir mantenerse alerta tras una jornada de 10 a 14 horas.

En caso de conflicto, un juez "flotante" juzgaría el trabajo. Para este menester había varios jueces "flotantes" disponibles en la sala de deliberación. Un conflicto surge cuando un juez se encuentra con un trabajo de su publicación, de una publicación para la cual ha hecho trabajo de consultoría recientemente (recientemente se define como un período de 18 meses inmediatamente previo al concurso) o de una publicación con la cual compite directamente. La Sociedad presenta cuatro niveles de premios:

El Premio a la Excelencia se otorga a un trabajo verdaderamente excelente. La habilidad meramente técnica o estética no debería reconocerse. Pero para recibir un premio estos trabajos no necesariamente tienen que ser "perfectos." Es apropiado honrar trabajos por cosas tales como ser innovador y osado si el trabajo es extraordinario pero no llega al 100 por ciento en todos los aspectos.

La Medalla de Bronce se otorga a trabajos que se sitúan por encima del Premio a la Excelencia. Puede otorgarse a cualquier trabajo que reciba tres votos en las discusiones sobre medallas del equipo de jueces. El dominio técnico de la Medalla de Bronce debería alcanzar los límites del medio.

La Medalla de Plata se otorga a trabajos que van más allá de la excelencia. El dominio técnico de la Medalla de Plata debería potenciar los límites del medio. Estos trabajos deben brillar.

La Medalla de Oro se otorga a trabajos que definen la perfección en la diciplina. Tales trabajos deben desafiar los límites de la creatividad. Debería ser imposible encontrar algo deficiente en un trabajo ganador de una medalla de oro.

Además de los Premios a la Excelencia y de las tres medallas, existen otros dos honores posibles: el Reconocimiento Especial del Juez y el premio al Mejor del Concurso. Estos honores son poco frecuentes y sólo se conceden cuando ciertas circunstancias específicas y especiales dan fundamento al premio.

Reconocimiento Especial del Juez: Este honor puede ser otorgado por un equipo de jueces o por todos los jueces a un trabajo que se destaca en un aspecto particular no descrito en la estructura del Premio a la Excelencia o de las medallas de Bronce, Plata y Oro. Este reconocimiento ha sido concedido por cosas tales como el uso de la fotografía, uso de material gráfico informativo y el uso de la tipografía a través de un conjunto de obras. Este conjunto de obras puede ser una publicación en particular, sección o secciones a cargo de un individuo o plantel. El reconocimiento especial no suplanta ningún Premio a la Excelencia o medalla de Bronce, Plata u Oro, y no debería considerarse como accesorio. En la jerarquía de los premios, encaja entre el nivel de la Medalla de Plata y la de Oro. Está claramente un eslabón por encima de la Medalla de Plata porque generalmente se concede por un conjunto de obras de excelencia uniforme, pero no alcanza la Medalla de Oro debido a la estrechez de su enfoque.

Mejor del Concurso: Como implica su nombre, éste es el mejor entre los ganadores de Medalla de Oro. Todas las discusiones para la concesión de este premio se llevan a cabo al concluir las deliberaciones. Los jueces han tenido ya la oportunidad de ver todos los ganadores de Plata y Oro al mismo tiempo. No hay límites en cuanto a la cantidad de premios al Mejor del Concurso que pueden presentarse en una o más categorías. Este año el premio al Mejor del Concurso fue otorgado al Miami Herald por su cobertura del Huracán Andrew.

It was the only story in South Florida for days after the storm. *The Miami Herald's* page 1 showed it: Overpowering headlines, big photographs, fewer stories, more pullout boxes and extensive keylines to inside stories. The dominant headlines ranged from 135 to 212 points.

A day before the storm, 50,000 copies of a special edition, headlined The Big One, were printed and distributed to hurricane shelters around Dade County. A tight production schedule resulted in the use of no color. Only hours after the hurricane hit, another special edition, with the first photos of the destruction, was distributed. Lack of water prevented the use of color for that issue and for the issue the following day. Without water, without air conditioning, without electricity to all the building, *The Herald* never missed an edition.

The Herald's breaking news entry comprised 255 pages, entered in three separate categories. The hurricane coverage won five Gold awards, five Silver awards and nine awards of excellence. It was this body of work that the judges selected for the 14th Edition's only Best of Show honor.

In the words of the judges:

The Best of Show is presented to the staff of *The Miami Herald* for its extraordinary presentation of its Hurricane Andrew report. Created and sustained through the most difficult of circumstances, it is an exemplary, content-driven package of compelling photography, smart infographics and thorough and thoughtful editing/reporting. It represents the highest achievement for teamwork within the newsroom, an achievement that sets a new standard for the newspaper community.

Al plantel de The Miami Herald por la extraordinaria presentación de sus crónicas sobre el Huracán Andrew. Creado y llevado a cabo en dificilísimas circunstancias, es un conjunto ejemplar impulsado por su contenido, de fotografía apremiante, gráficas informativas inteligentes, y crónicas y redacción profundas y exhaustivas. Representa el logro más alto de un equipo dentro de una sala de noticias, un logro que marca un nuevo estándar para la comunidad de los periódicos.

Best of Show Credits

The Miami Herald
News Desk: Herschel Kenner, Daryl Kannberg, Mary Behne, Mel Frishman, Ed McDonald, Frank Davies, Dennis Fitzgerald, Rory Clarke

Local desk: Bill Grueskin, Pete Rice, Bob Radziewicz, Rick Hirsch, Tim White, Ronnie Ramos and Justin Gillis

Broward News Desk: Joe Ames, Kurt Gardner, Mike Judge, Harry Broertjes, Joe Modzelewski, David Hinds, David Blasco

State Desk: John Pancake, Mark Washburn, Greg Melikov

Sports Desk: Bill Grant

Business Desk: Rex Seline, Jim Watters, Brad Lehman, Daisey Harris

Neighbors Desk: Maria Garcia, Tracy Grant, Connie Ogle, Lorraine Welsch and George Haj

Home & Design/Home

Buying: Max Roberts, Diane Kolyer, Jill Cassidy, Kathy Foster, Dale DuPont

Features Desk: Steve Sonsky, Elissa Vanaver, Rhonda Prast, Herman Vega, Lynn Medford, Kendall Hamersly, Emily Hathaway

Diversions: Dave Hogerty

Graphics Desk: Roman Lyskowski, John Van Beekum, Shelly Bowen, Bill Andrews, Ramon Dejesus, Jose Iglesias, David Walters, Battle Vaughan

Photography Staff: Candace Barbot, Albert Coya, Tim Chapman, Maurice Cohn-Band, Al Diaz, Bob Eighmie, Chuck Fadely, Pat Farrell, Bill Frakes, G.W. Griffin, Carlos Guerrero, A. Brennan Innerarity, Carl Juste, Jon Kral, Rick McCawley, Peter Portilla, Joe Rimkus Jr., Jeffery Salter, Mike Stocker, Dezso Szuri, Charlie Trainor Jr.

Editorial Artists: Rick Brownlee, Patterson Clark,

Dan Clifford, Phill Flanders, Roy Gallup, Bert Garcia, Tiffany Grantham, Liz Heisler, Hiram Henriquez, Ana Lense-Larrauri, Alex Leary, Reggie Myers, Terrance Oliver, Pam Swischer, Woody Vondracek

Graphics/Design Interns: Julio Fernandez, Dan Gonzalez, Derek Hembd, Juan Lopez, Robert Miller, Danielle Parks

Also:

Doug Clifton, Executive Editor;

Pete Weitzel, Managing Editor;

Susan Olds, Ileana Oroza, Sue Reisinger, Joe Oglesby, Wayne Markham, Assistant Managing Editors;

Dennis Copeland, Director of Photography;

Steve Rice, AME/ Graphics;

Randy Stano, Director/Editorial Art & Design

Gold & Best of Show
The Miami Herald
Staff

SPECIAL HURRICANE EDITION

The Miami Herald

MONDAY, AUGUST 24, 1992 · CONTENTS COPYRIGHT © 1992 THE MIAMI HERALD · 25 CENTS

AN AWFUL HOWL

Andrew hits hardest in South Dade

At least two dead; 5,000 left homeless

Entire region suffers damage

By ARNOLD MARKOWITZ
Herald Staff Writer

Hurricane Andrew, the most fearsome storm to hit South Florida in decades, howled ashore early today with 138-mile-an-hour winds, killing at least two and leaving a path of destruction from Fort Lauderdale to the Florida Keys.

Complacency, growing almost without interruption since the last major hurricane hit the southeast coast in 1965, fell down with uncountable trees, power lines and assorted debris.

Five thousand people were left homeless by the storm, Metro Police Director Fred Taylor announced. They'll be moved into shelters in North Dade.

Taylor declared parts of South Dade a restricted area, meaning people are prohibited from going in.

The hurricane's center slashed ashore 28 miles south of downtown Miami, went ripping through the suburbs around a pulsating eye nearly 20 miles across. The strongest gust recorded, before 4 a.m. when instruments at the National Hurricane Center in Coral Gables were blown out of commission,

PLEASE SEE ANDREW, 3

NOT MUCH LEFT: Vidal Martinez hid in a laundry room this morning as the hurricane chewed through the trailer park he lives in near U.S. 1 and Southwest 124th St.

C.W. GRIFFIN / Miami Herald Staff

HURRICANE

A NOTE FROM THE PUBLISHER

Among the great traditions of newspapering is an Extra edition. It is quite rare, used almost always only with news events of great moment. This past day, these past hours, furnish such a moment.

You will find 28 pages, in English and in Spanish, focusing on the power of Hurricane Andrew and the pain of those in its path.

In the neighborhoods of our community, people already have emerged to marvel and often weep at the damage and to begin the task of rebuilding.

You can already feel the spirit of a community that will use this occasion to come closer together.

Hundreds of Herald and El Nuevo Herald people were at their posts, sleeping at most fitfully, through the fearsome night to be able to bring you this special edition.

By tomorrow, we hope to be able to return to our regular schedule of newspapers delivered to homes as well as available elsewhere.

Dave Lawrence

RUMOR CONTROL NUMBERS
■ Dade: 596-4735
■ Broward: 357-6464
■ Palm Beach: 407-233-3500
■ Key West: 294-9981
■ Middle Keys: 743-7986
■ Upper Keys: 664-4039

FURY OVER MIAMI

The center of Hurricane Andrew passes just south of Miami, in a satellite photo taken about 5 a.m. today. Sustained winds were clocked at 138 mph around the 20-mile-wide eye of the storm, and the worst damage appeared to be in Dade below Kendall Drive.

Associated Press / CNN

ANDREW'S FURY
9 pages of coverage
3-11

FACTS AND FIGURES
■ **Death toll** (unconfirmed): 2 in Miami, 4 in the Bahamas.
■ **Casualties:** Unknown.
■ **Damage:** Property damage severe in South Dade, Kendall and Coral Gables. Trees down throughout region. Many roads impassable because of debris.
■ **Landfall of eye:** 4:52 a.m., near Homestead.
■ **Strength of storm:** Gusts up to 164 mph, sustained winds of 140 mph, a Category 4 storm.
■ **Residents evacuated:** 700,000.
■ **Those seeking refuge in shelters:** 90,000.
■ **Customers without power:** 1.3 million.

INDEX

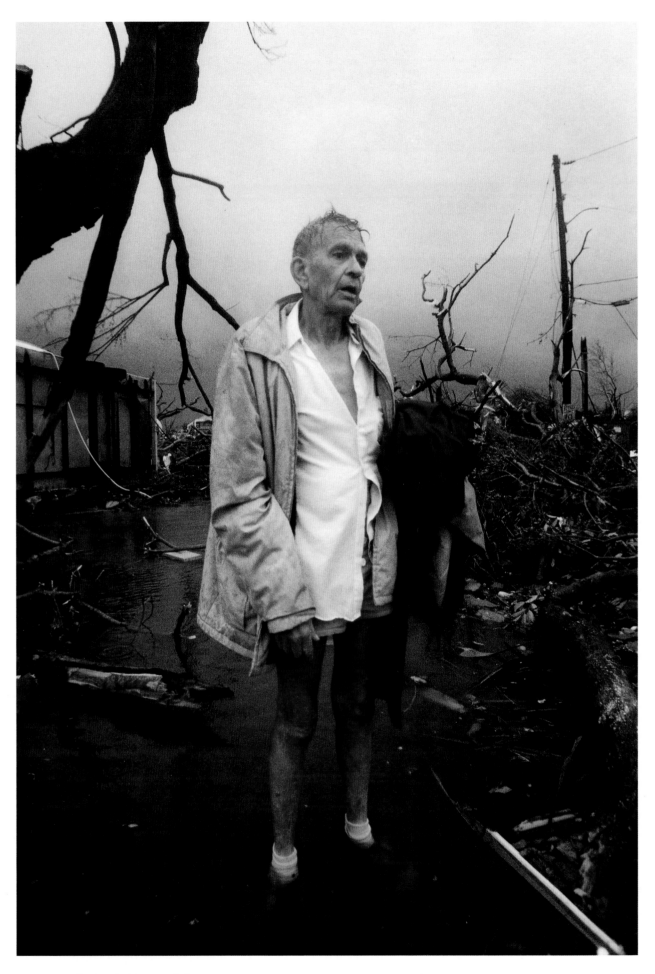

Gold & Best of Show
The Miami Herald
C.M. Guerrero, Photographer; Dennis Copeland, Director of Photography; Steve Rice, AME Graphics

BEST OF SHOW

Gold & Best of Show
The Miami Herald
Staff

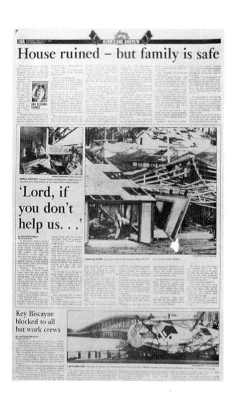

8 THE BEST OF NEWSPAPER DESIGN

THURSDAY, Aug. 27

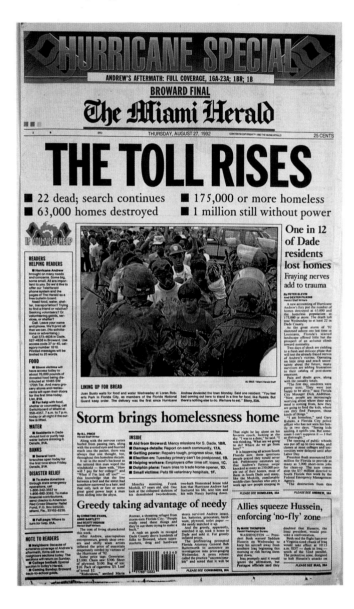

Gold & Best of Show
The Miami Herald

Herschel Kenner, News Staff; Daryl Kannberg, News Staff;
Mary Behne, News Staff; Mel Frishman, News Staff; Dennis
Copeland, Photo Director; Roman Lyskowski, Photo Staff;
Woody Vondracek, Graphics Artist; Hiram Henriquez,
Graphics Artist; Steve Rice, AME Graphics; Randy Stano,
Director/Editorial Art & Design

FRIDAY, Aug. 28

SATURDAY, Aug. 29

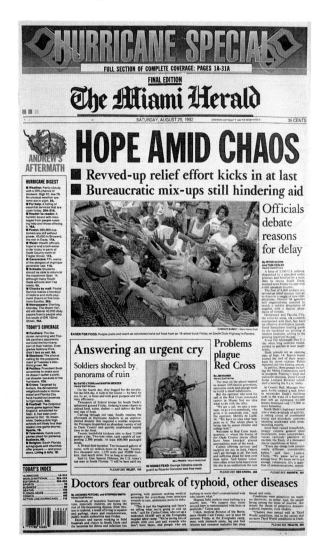

SUNDAY, Aug. 30

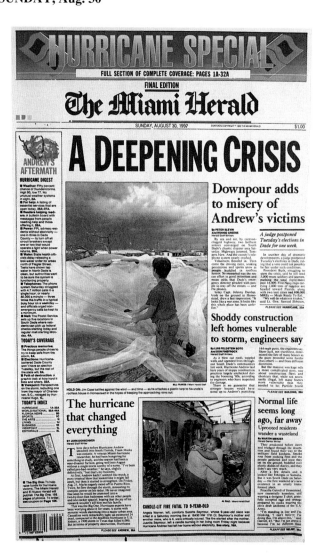

MONDAY, Aug. 31

TUESDAY, Sept. 1

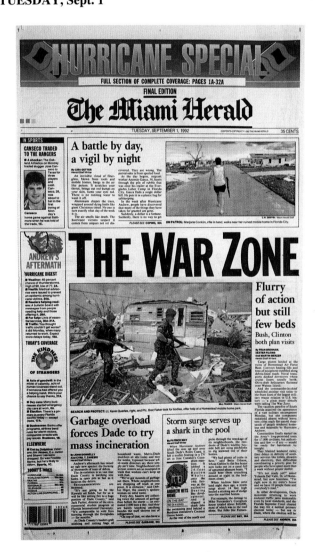

Silver

The Miami Herald

Dan Clifford, Graphics Editor; Stephen K. Doig, Research
Editor; Daryl Kannberg, Staff Writer; Jeff Leen, National
Editor; Randy Stano, Director/Editorial Art & Design

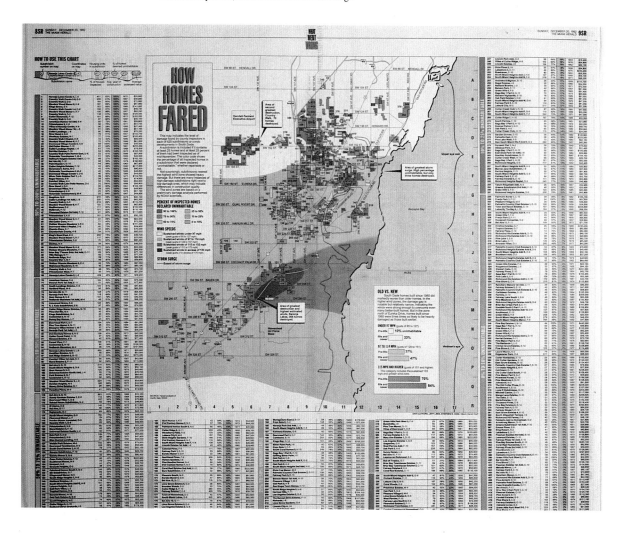

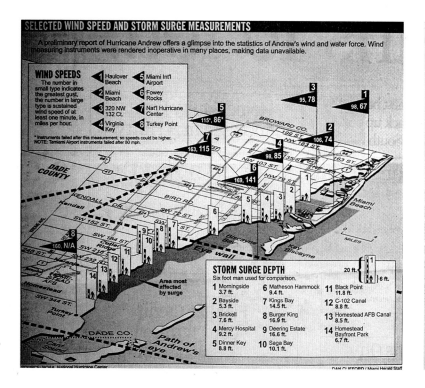

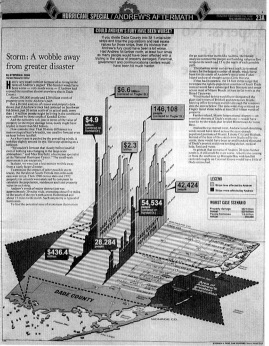

Silver

The Miami Herald

Dan Clifford, Graphics Editor; Stephen K. Doig, Research Editor; Jeff Leen, Staff Writer; Daryl Kannberg, News Editor/Broward; Randy Stano, Director/Editorial Art & Design

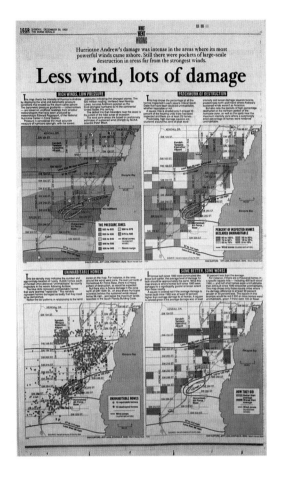

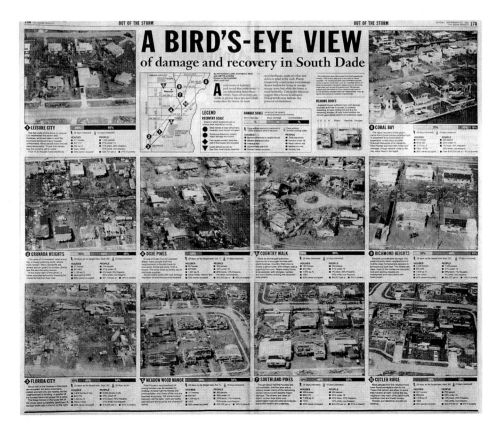

Silver

The Miami Herald

Patterson Clark, Graphics Artist; Randy Stano, Director/Editorial Art & Design; Tim Chapman, Photographer; Stephen K. Doig, Reporter; Lizette Alvarez, Reporter

Silver
The Miami Herald

Dan Clifford, Graphics Editor; Randy Stano,
Director/Editorial Art & Design

Silver
The Miami Herald

Reginald Myers, Graphics Artist; Pat May, Researcher;
Rich Hirsch, Assistant Local Editor; Randy Stano,
Director/Editorial Art & Design

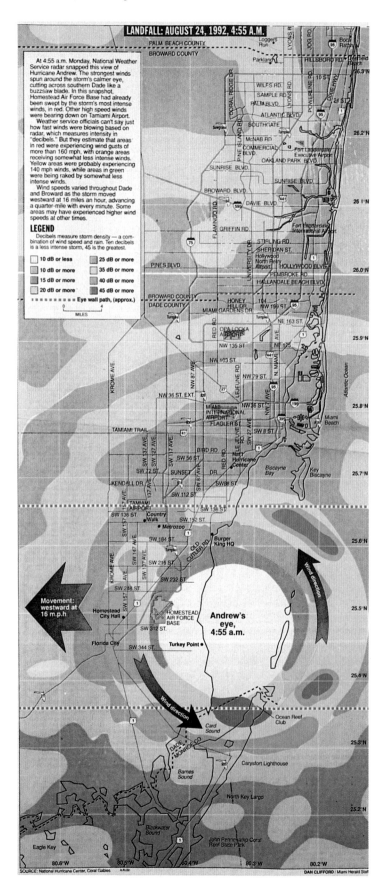

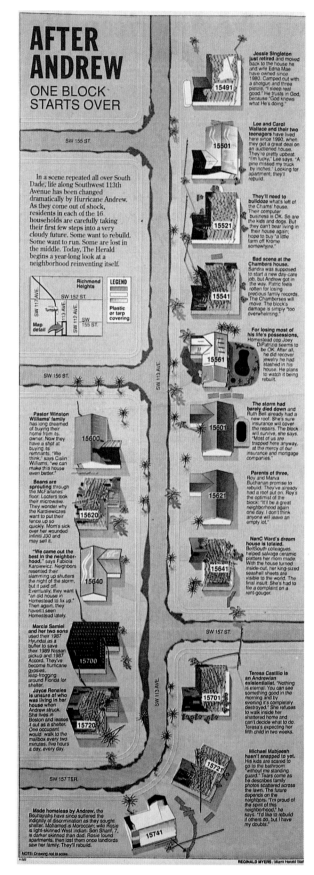

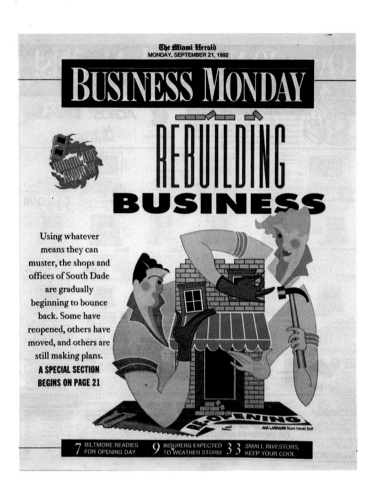

The Miami Herald
MONDAY, SEPTEMBER 21, 1992

BUSINESS MONDAY

REBUILDING BUSINESS

Using whatever means they can muster, the shops and offices of South Dade are gradually beginning to bounce back. Some have reopened, others have moved, and others are still making plans.

A SPECIAL SECTION BEGINS ON PAGE 21

7 BILTMORE READIES FOR OPENING DAY **9** INSURERS EXPECTED TO WEATHER STORM **33** SMALL INVESTORS, KEEP YOUR COOL

Silver
The Miami Herald

Ana Lense-Larrauri, Illustrator & Designer; Jim Watters, Business Monday News Editor; Rex Seline, Executive Business Editor; Randy Stano, Director/Editorial Art & Design

Award of Excellence
The Miami Herald

Jon Kral, Photographer; Dennis Copeland, Director of Photography; Steve Rice, AME Graphics

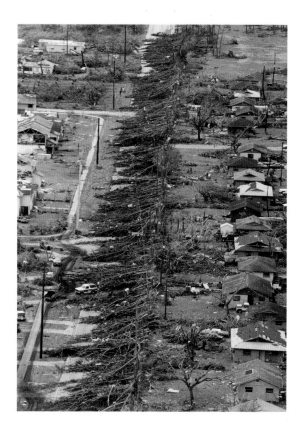

Gold & Best of Show
The Miami Herald
Staff

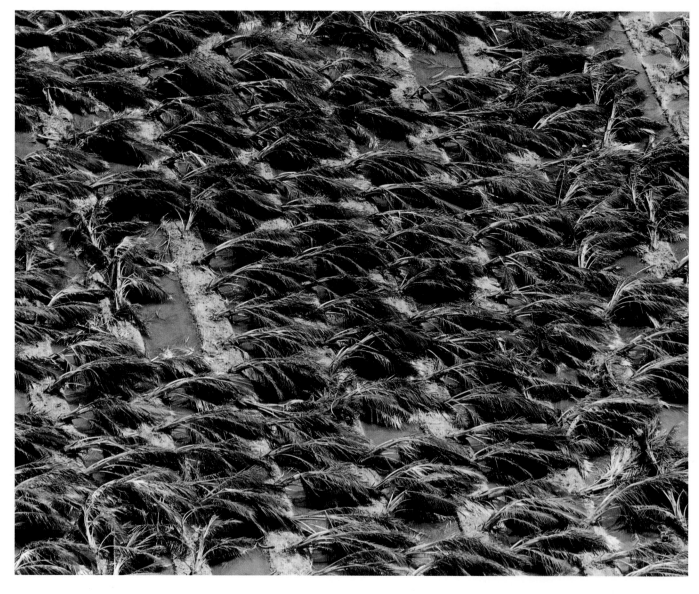

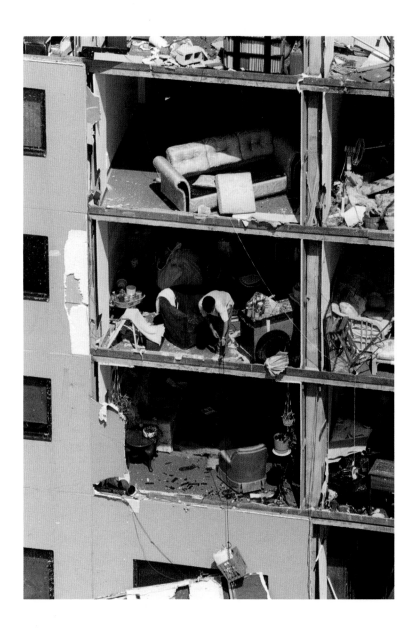

Gold & Best of Show
The Miami Herald
Staff

Award of Excellence

The Miami Herald

Alex Leary, Graphics Artist; Juan Lopez, Designer; Max
Roberts, Section Editor; Randy Stano, Director/Editorial
Art & Design

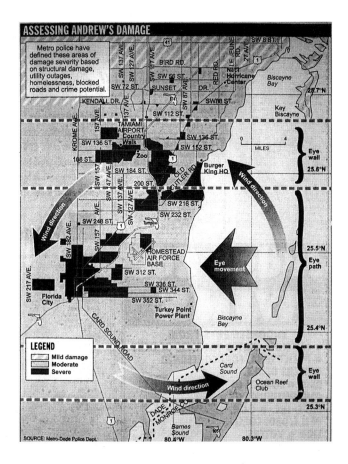

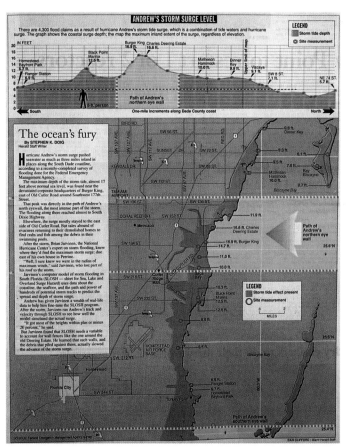

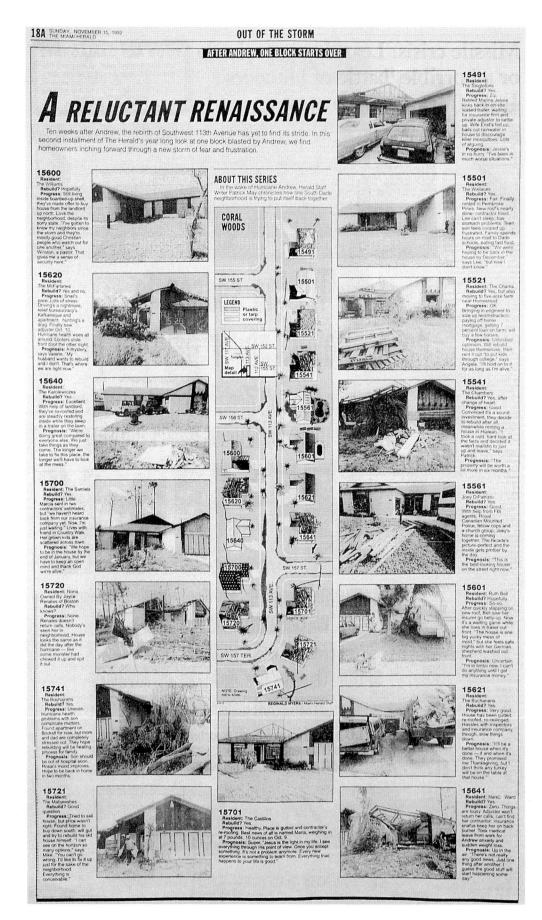

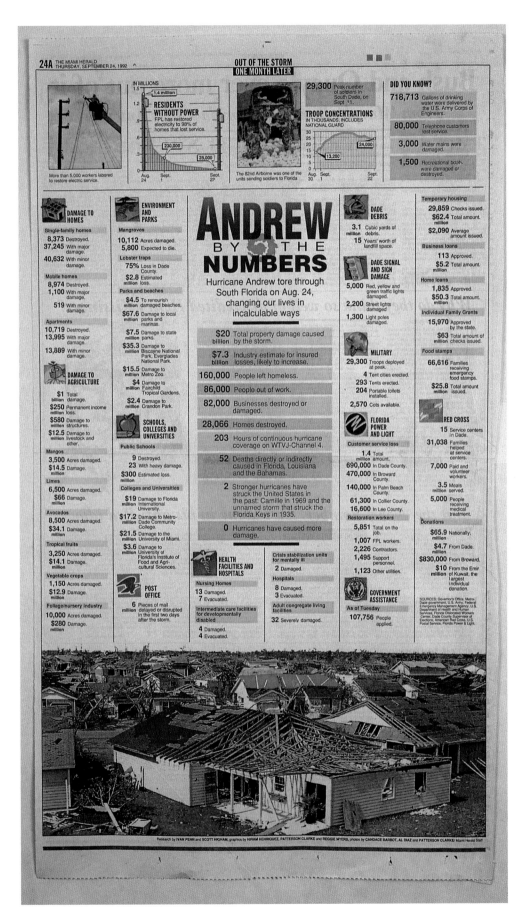

Award of Excellence

The Miami Herald

Hiram Henriquez, Graphics Artist; Patterson Clark, Graphics Artist; Reggie Myers, Graphics Artist; Ivan Penn, Researcher; Scott Higham, Researcher; Candice Barbot, Photographer; Al Diaz, Photographer; Randy Stano, Director/Editorial Art & Design

Award of Excellence

The Boston Globe

Staff

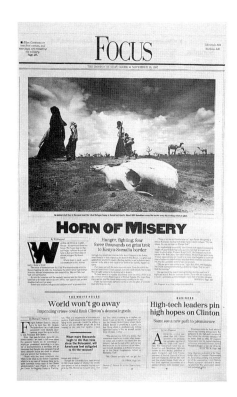

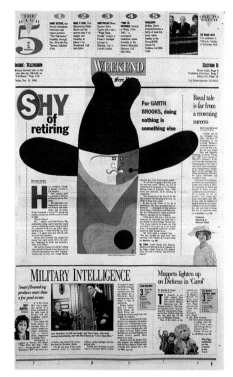

Award of Excellence

Detroit Free Press

Staff

Award of Excellence
The Detroit News
Staff

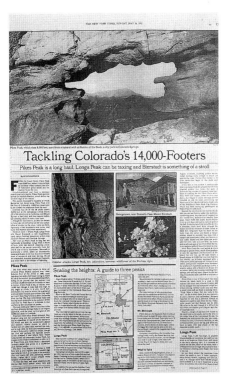

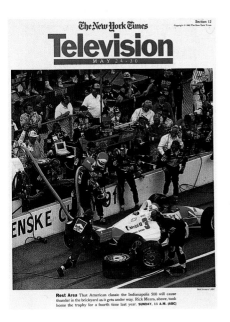

Award of Excellence
The New York Times
Tom Bodkin, Design Director; Staff

Award of Excellence

The Oregonian

Portland, OR

Tim Harrower, Designer; Mark Wigginton, Art Director;
Staff Designers

Award of Excellence

The Christian Science Monitor

Staff

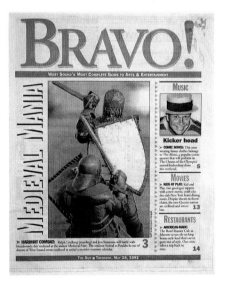

Award of Excellence

The Sun

Bremerton, WA

Scott Whitcomb, Designer

Award of Excellence

Eastsideweek

Kirkland, WA

Sandra Schneider, Art Director;
Staff; Freelance Artists

Love in the time of Clearasil

A surprise summer-before-college couple beat the stereotypes on Mercer Island

By Greg Palmer

When Ray Kroc took over McDonald's back in the '50s and began looking for a great grinning workforce to do his bidding and frying, his restaurants were not allowed to hire women. Kroc thought teen-age girls behind the counter whose interest in teen-age girls far surpassed their interest in cheap burgers.

These young men would hang around the Golden Arches, drooling but not eating, and thus drive away business—not a desirable situation when you have billions and billions of burgers to unload. Or so Mr. Kroc believed.

Irma, the owner of Mercer Island's Samoa Drive-In a decade later, had no such theories. When an opening occurred on the Samoa team roster, Irma hired the first reasonably clean person who asked for the job and looked like he or she could do it. Thus she hired me in the spring of '65 to be a cook. Perhaps Irma sensed that I was not the type to attract drooling teen females. If so, she was kind and didn't mention it.

So the Samoa did employ women, such as Arlene the Weekday Counter Personnel. Lads did not lust for Arlene. Though attractive in her way, she was ancient—at least 30—and a single mother who had already seen enough teen males to last her the rest of her life. She didn't take any crap from anybody, and once offered to "box the ears" of an All-Conference tackle if he "opened his big mouth one more time." He didn't.

The other regular female Samoa employee was Deedee, a junior collegian from Kirkland who worked nights and weekends and was the first person I ever saw who put her hair up in rollers made from orange-juice cans. (Arlene had a problem with this.) It would have been easy for us teen males to work up a sweat over the worldly Deedee, except that her massive college boyfriend could show up at any time, and did; he was an impressive argument for a cold shower.

On the other side of the counter, there were a few women who lingered longer than they had to. To be a teen female known for hanging around the Samoa was not the way to get elected to Mercer Girls, but the Samoa Girls wouldn't have wanted any part of that anyway.

They were content to sit on car hoods or in the booths smoking and giggling, swapping quips with the boys who were their counterparts and semi-constant companions. They traded these young men back and forth as boyfriends the way they traded Barbie Doll clothing throughout the previous decade.

If this crowd seemed to be more sexually active than most Eastside teens, they still had their own strict moral code, such as never stealing somebody else's mate unless they're about to break up anyway, doing it either with off-island guys or with off-island guys but never both, nor describing your sexual conquests to anyone other than your closest nine or ten friends, and finally, never messing around outside your social class.

Social class for island teens back then was not based on parental income. Among those who hung out at the Samoa were people from families worth millions, and people from families that still did a little truck farming in their back yard to make ends meet. But such financial disparity meant nothing. What separated us was brains, or more accurately, how you applied the brains you had. To be an official layabout Samoan you had to refer to all teachers as "Old Man Smith" or "Old Lady Jones," correctly distinguish between automobile makes and engine sizes at long distances, and hang out at the Samos.

(It is only fair to mention that these layabouts included a future airline pilot, wildlife artist, automobile designer, restaurateur, three highly decorated Marines, a poet, two excellent mothers, and the first unlimited hydroplane driver since Joe Taggart who could speak in complete sentences. These were not dumb people, just motivation-impaired.)

Perhaps, in their couplings and recouplings, true love bloomed amongst them, but mostly I think it was just exploratory lust. Love was an extremely rare commodity at the Samos, which is why the only time it occurred that summer still lingers in the memory like root-beer residue on the side of a mug.

He was one of our regulars, a lanky young man with thick brown hair who hadn't quite found himself, and hadn't found anybody else, either. Very quiet most of the time, when he made any sound at all it was usually a laugh like Goofy's, a "guh-hilk guh-hilk" that

• Sam Neill plays a chef in a sleazy rock 'n' roll club who gets tainted by drug dealing and murder in *Death in Brunswick*. At Metro.

Movies

BY TOM KEOGH
and others as noted

Openings

Candyman—My college nickname has been co-opted for this film adaptation of a Clive Barker horror story (just kidding). Virginia Madsen stars in this tale of a fabled demon who can be summoned by calling his name three times. *Starts 10/16, theater TBA.*

Consenting Adults—The Two Kevins (Kline and Spacey) star as a couple of yuppie neighbors who swap wives, one of whom ends up dead. With Forest Whitaker. Directed by Alan J. Pakula (*Klute*), who needs to make a really good film again. Maybe this is it. *Starts 10/16 at Crossroads, Kirkland Parkplace.*

L'Elegante Criminel—Daniel Auteuil portrays 19th-century rogue and seducer Lacenaire, a prominent character in the classic *Children of Paradise*. Lacenaire is charged with murder, precipitating an enormous press event. *Starts 10/16 at Neptune.*

Feed—An odd documentary by Kevin Rafferty and James Ridgeway that circles some kind of point for 70-odd minutes, but never quite lands. Compiled of video clips of various 1992 presidential candidates fussing, joking, and snarling off into the electronic void before on-air interviews, the film gives equal time to making everyone from Harkin to Buchanan look like an idiot. There are plenty of funny scenes in this film, and many horrible ones, particularly in original footage of the candidates coming face-to-face with a daily freak show from among the electorate. We blush about these public figures constantly, but one has to wonder why they don't retire out of Swiftian repulsion with the human race. Anyway, *Feed*, at its best, leans toward a kind of dismantling of the media apparatus that creates personas and images, and it has elements of an interesting, experimental "found" work of cinema. It also leaves one thinking about a strange media disconnection where alternate lives exist within outtakes and sound checks, none of which average Americans ever see or hear. But the film is also awry and only slightly more relevant than an average segment of *Not Necessarily The News*. *Starts 10/16 at Metro.*

Calendarweek is a selective listing of arts, entertainment, and other activities on the Eastside and environs. With last-minutes (or post-deadline) changes common in the entertainment world, we recommend calling ahead to verify dates, times, and locations. To be eligible for inclusion in Calendarweek, written descriptions of events must be received no later than **Thursday at noon** of the week prior to publication (*Eastsideweek* is published every Wednesday). Calendarweek is prepared by Helen Gould and Matthew Flaugh. Send information to Calendarweek, *Eastsideweek*, 123 Lake St. N, Suite B-1, Kirkland, WA 98011.

CONTINUED ON PAGE 32

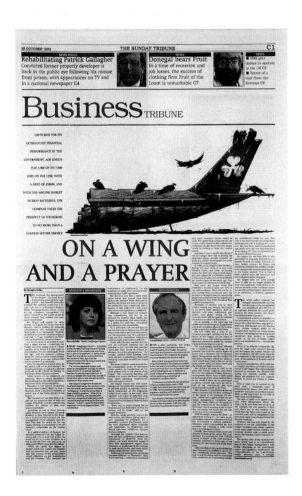

Award of Excellence

The Sunday Tribune

Dublin, Ireland

Vincent Browne, Editor; Stephen Ryan, Design
Editor/Photo Editor; Paul Hopkins, Production Editor;
Ger Siggins, Sports Editor; Con O'Midheach, Copy
Editor; Tom Vavasour, Production Manager; Frank
Dolan, Systems Manager

Bronze
The Detroit News
Dale Peskin, AME; Christy Bradford,
ME; James Gatti, Deputy ME; Frank
Lovinski, Assistant ME; Sue Burzynski,
Assistant ME; Nancy Hanus, Assistant
NE; Joe Gray, Assistant NE; Beth
Valone, Assistant NE; Bob Howard,
Designer & Copy Editor; Felecia
Henderson, Designer & Copy Editor

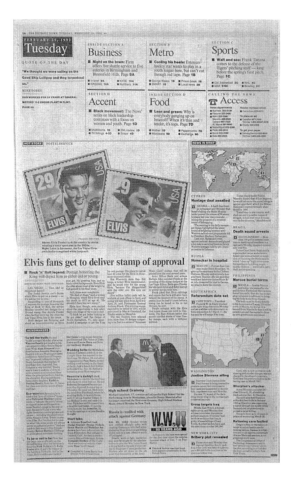

Award of Excellence
Detroit Free Press
Wayne Kamidoi, Designer; Ken McDonald, Designer;
Sue Parker, Designer; Lee Yarosh, Designer; Deborah
Withey, Design Director; Joe Zeff, Designer

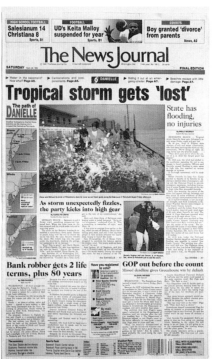

Award of Excellence
Maine Sunday Telegram
Portland, ME
Bob Dixon, Copy Desk Chief; Andrea Philbrick, Design
Editor; Rick Wakely, Graphics Editor

Award of Excellence
The News Journal
Wilmington, DE
Staff

Award of Excellence
The Orange County Register
Santa Ana, CA
Staff

Award of Excellence
San Jose Mercury News

Bryan Monroe, Design Director; David Yarnold, Deputy
Managing Editor; Jeff Thomas, Executive News Editor;
Sue Morrow, Picture Editor; Susan Steade, News Editor;
Molly Swisher, Art Director; Mike Mayer, News Editor;
Sam Hundley, Features Design Director

Award of Excellence
The Washington Times

Michael Keating, AME/News; Joseph Scopin, AME
Graphics; Don Renfroe, News Editor; Greg Pierce,
Assistant News Editor; Greg Groesch, Art Director; Alex
Gonzalez, Artist; Henry Christopher, Artist; Jim Fiedler,
Photo Director

Award of Excellence
The Ann Arbor News

Ann Arbor, MI
Staff

Award of Excellence
Chicago Tribune

Nancy J. Canfield, Design Director; Marjorie David,
Editor; Lee Behrens, Assistant Editor; Staff
Photographers

Award of Excellence
The Daily Telegraph

London, England
Staff

Award of Excellence
Gazette Telegraph

Colorado Springs, CO
Dan Cotter, Designer; Tim Filby, Designer

Award of Excellence
The Times-Picayune

New Orleans, LA

Billy Turner, Assistant Sports Editor; Staff

Award of Excellence
The Washington Times

George Kolb, Sports Layout Editor; Montgomery Wood, Designer

Award of Excellence
The Citizen

Auburn, NY

Gary Piccirillo, AME Design

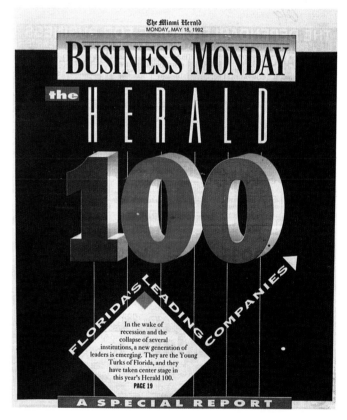

Silver
The Miami Herald

Ana Lense-Larrauri, Illustrator & Designer; Jim Watters, Business Monday News Editor;
Rex Seline, Executive Business Editor; Randy Stano, Director/Editorial Art & Design

Silver

San Bernardino County Sun

San Bernardino, CA

Rosemary McClure, AME; Larry Nista, Copy Editor; Betts Griffone, Graphics Editor;
Patrick Olsen, News Editor; John Weeks, Assistant Features Editor

Gold

The Orange County Register

Santa Ana, CA

Brenda Shoun, Assistant News Editor/Design; Claudia Guerrero, Designer; Nadia Borowski, Photographer; Pam Marshak, Assistant Topic Editor; Kevin Byrne, News Editor/Design; Nanette Bisher, AME/Art Director; Larry Burroughs, Assistant Managing Editor; Ana Venegas, Photographer; Chris Carlson, Photo Editor; Jay Bryant, Photo Editor

Award of Excellence
Chicago Tribune

Stephen Ravenscraft, Art Director; Therese Shechter, Designer; Tony Majeri, Senior Design Director; Celeste Schaefer, Designer; Stephen Cvengros, Editor

Gold

The Atlanta Journal/Constitution

Renee Hannans, Photographer; Mike Gordon, Design
Director; Tony De Feria, Art Director; Ron Feinberg, Editor

WEATHER

Sunny
Today's high, 82
Overnight low, 60
Weather report, G10
•••
News index, A2

THE ATLANTA CONSTITUTION

THURSDAY, OCTOBER 15, 1992

SPORTS FINAL

NATIONAL LEAGUE CHAMPIONS

OH, YES!

Braves rally for incredible 9th-inning win

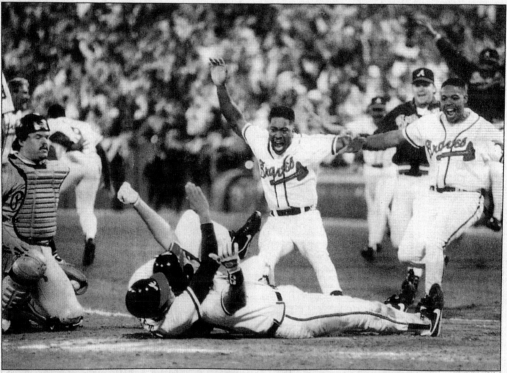

RENEE HANNANS / Staff

Victory rush: The Braves run out to embrace Sid Bream, who lies at home plate after scoring the winning run Wednesday. Bream avoided the tag of Pirate catcher Mike Lavalliere (left).

Fans erupt in joy as Game 7 heroics send team back to World Series

By I.J. Rosenberg and A. R. Tays
STAFF WRITERS

Slow-footed Sid Bream slid across home plate late Wednesday night, capping one of the most dramatic comebacks in the history of American sports and giving the Braves their second straight National League title.

"God bless Atlanta. Oh my God, unbelievable!" shouted Bob Huntey, a Chamblee salesman who was hugging his wife, Sylvia, as he watched Bream come across the plate.

The end of the NL Championship Series came at 11:53 p.m. amid pandemonium both inside and outside the stadium. The crowd of 51,975, already at a fever pitch, erupted. Players, TV crews, photographers, security

personnel and mounted policemen rushed onto the field, where the Braves players were piling on top of Bream, whose slide beat Barry Bonds's throw and the lunging tag attempt of catcher Mike LaValliere.

By 1 a.m., the streets of Buckhead were in bedlam. Fans did the tomahawk chop from atop traffic lights, buildings and billboards.

The celebration started after the Braves, trailing the entire game, rallied for three runs in the bottom of the ninth inning to eclipse the Pittsburgh Pirates, 3-2.

The come-from-behind win belonged to Francisco Cabrera, who hit a two-out line drive to left field, sending David Justice and Bream across the plate.

The victory clinched the Braves' second

straight NL pennant four games to three and sends them on to face the American League champion Toronto Blue Jays in the World Series, which will begin Saturday night in Atlanta.

In Buckhead, thousands of people poured out of the bars. Wasa Zaida, 30, of Pakistan was sitting on top of a car as it crawled through the crowd.

"We're winners! We're winners! We're winners!" he shouted, shaking his fist.

"We're raising hell because we went into the depths of defeat and we really thought we lost it," said Jeff Brown, 24, of Marietta who now owes his girlfriend five nights out at $100 a night because he was sure Atlanta would lose.

"We're in a total shock," said Cardin Mixon, 26 of Atlanta. "We sat stressed out for eight-and-a-half innings. We concentrated. We wouldn't let anyone leave their seats."

With the crack of Cabrera's bat, a roar went up in Athens, home of the University of Georgia. People burst out of their houses and ran screaming toward Milledge Avenue, where fraternity brothers were chanting on their front lawns and flagging passing cars — their horns blaring — with tomahawk chops.

In downtown Athens, a crowd watching the Braves game on the big screen at the Georgia Theatre burst into the street,

Please see **BRAVES, A5** ▶

● INSIDE: Complete coverage of the game and fans / SPORTS, SECTION E

Bronze

The Albuquerque Tribune

Lara Edge, Designer; Mike Davis, Picture Editor

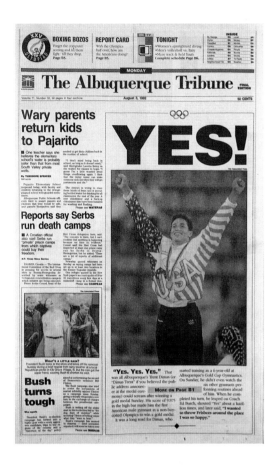

Silver

Detroit Free Press

Wayne Kamidoi, Designer

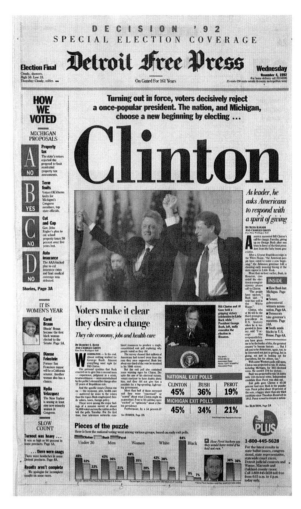

Bronze

Houston Press

Audrey Satterwhite, Art Director; Phillip Burke, Illustrator; Chris Hearne, Publisher; John Wilburn, Editor

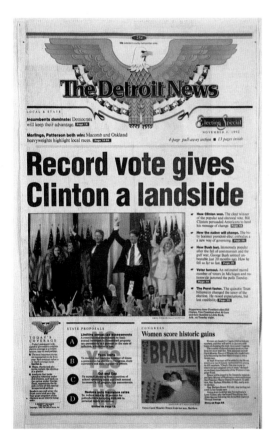

Bronze

The Detroit News

Dale Peskin, AME; Robert Graham, Art Director & Illustrator

Award of Excellence

The Albuquerque Tribune

Lara Edge, Designer; Mike Gallegos, Photo Editor;
Randall K. Roberts, AME Graphics

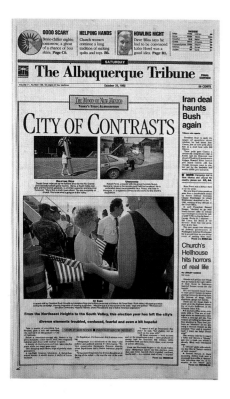

Award of Excellence

The Albuquerque Tribune

Lara Edge, Designer; Eric Draper, Photo Editor; Anita
Baca, Photographer

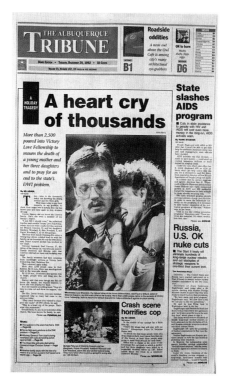

Award of Excellence

The Ann Arbor News

Ann Arbor, MI

Staff

Award of Excellence

El Mundo Deportivo

Barcelona, Spain

Toni Cases, Art Director; Jian Corbera, Sub Director

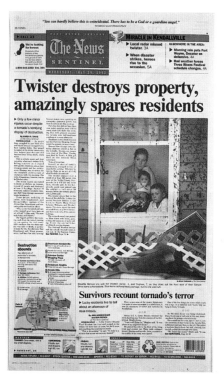

Award of Excellence

The News-Sentinel

Fort Wayne, IN

Dan Suwyn, Design Director; Tom Bissett, Designer;
Cindy Jones-Hulfachor, Graphics Reporter; Brian
Tombaugh, Photographer

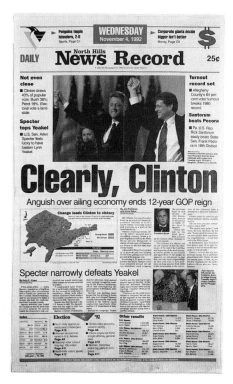

Award of Excellence

North Hills News Record

Warrendale, PA

Christopher J. Kozlowski, Presentation Editor; Saed
Hindash, Photographer

Award of Excellence
Anchorage Daily News

Mike Campbell, Designer & AME/Graphics; Ron Engstrom, Illustrator & Researcher; Leon Unruh, Copy Editor & Designer; David Hulen, Researcher

Award of Excellence
Austin American-Statesman

G.W. Babb, Design Director & Designer

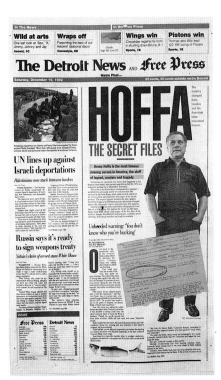

Award of Excellence
The Clarion-Ledger

Jackson, MS

Earnest Hart, Graphics Director & Designer; Frank Brown, Page One Editor; Scott Boyd, Photo Editor; Greg Jenson, Photographer; Tom Roster, Photographer

Award of Excellence
Dagens Nyheter

Stockholm, Sweden

Thomas Hall, Designer

Award of Excellence
Detroit Free Press

Deborah Withey, Design Director & Designer; Wayne Kamidoi, Designer

Award of Excellence

The Detroit News

Dale Peskin, AME; Joe Gray, Assistant News Editor

Award of Excellence

The Detroit News

Dale Peskin, AME; Joe Gray, Designer

Award of Excellence

The Detroit News

Dale Peskin, AME; Dierck Casselman, AME
Graphics/Design

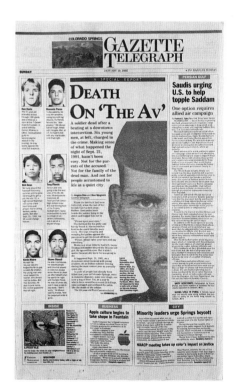

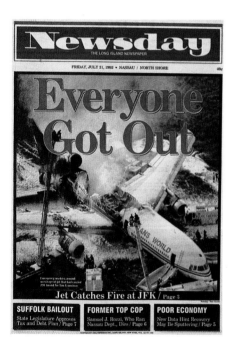

Award of Excellence

Gazette Telegraph

Colorado Springs, CO

Dan Cotter, Designer

Award of Excellence

La Vanguardia

Barcelona, Spain

Carlos Perez de Rozas, Art Director; Josep Rovirosa,
Graphic Design Editor; Josep Alberola, Graphic Design
Editor

Award of Excellence

Newsday

Daniel van Benthuysen, Senior Art Director; Doug
Wolfson, News Editor; Bob Brandt, ME; Stan Honda,
Photographer

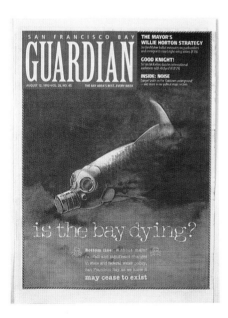

Award of Excellence
San Jose Mercury News

Sue Morrow, Designer & Picture Editor; Jeff Thomas, Executive News Editor; David Yarnold, Deputy ME; Bryan Monroe, Design Director; Jim Gensheimer, Photographer

Award of Excellence
St. Petersburg Times

Ron Reason, Designer; Trich Redman, Art Director

Award of Excellence
St. Petersburg Times

Ron Reason, Designer; Neville Green, Managing Editor

Award of Excellence
The Sunday Tribune

Dublin, Ireland

Stephen Ryan, Design Editor & Designer; Paul Hipkins, Production Editor; Associated Press Photographer

Award of Excellence
The Sunday Tribune

Dublin, Ireland

Stephen Ryan, Design Editor & Designer; Paul Hipkins, Production Editor; John Carlos, Photographer

Award of Excellence
The Sunday Tribune

Dublin, Ireland

Stephen Ryan, Design Editor & Designer; Paul Hipkins, Production Editor

Award of Excellence
The Virginian-Pilot
Norfolk, VA

Jeff Glick, Art Director; Brian Stallcop, Layout Editor; Pamela Smith-Rodden, News Editor; Latane Jones, Photo Editor; Alex Burrows, Photo Editor; Cole Campbell, ME; Sandra M. Rowe, Executive Editor; John Earle, Graphics Artist; Nelson Brown, Deputy ME/Presentation; Bob Lynn, AME Graphics

Award of Excellence
The Wichita Eagle
Wichita, KS

Alice Sky, News Editor/Visuals; Richard Crowson, Editorial Cartoonist

Award of Excellence
The Times-Picayune
New Orleans, LA

Beth Aguillard, Designer; Kurt Mutchler, Graphics Editor; George Berke, Design Director; Tom Gregory, Associate Editor

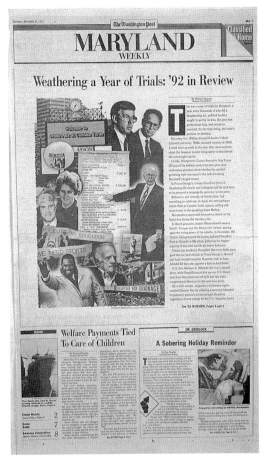

Silver
The Washington Post

Michael Keegan, AME; Carol Porter, Art Director & Layout Editor; Mason McAllister, Layout Editor; Jane Ashley, Layout Editor; Randy Mays, Illustrator

Award of Excellence

Calgary Herald

Calgary, Alberta, Canada

Rob Dudley, Senior Artist; Joe Hvilivitzky, Researcher/Writer; Mike Dempster, Editor; Dick Wallace, Art Director

Award of Excellence

The Record

Hackensack, NJ

Kevin O'Neil, Graphics Artist

Award of Excellence

The Record

Hackensack, NJ

Kevin O'Neil, Graphics Artist

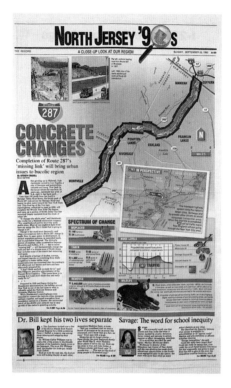

Award of Excellence

The Washington Post

Eileen Sisk, Design Editor; Kitty Chism, Editor

Award of Excellence

The Washington Post

Michael Keegan, AME; Carol Porter, Art Director/Layout Editor; Tim Clark, Illustrator; David McLimans, Illustrator

Silver

The Detroit News

Don Asmussen, Artist; Felix Grabowski, Graphics Director

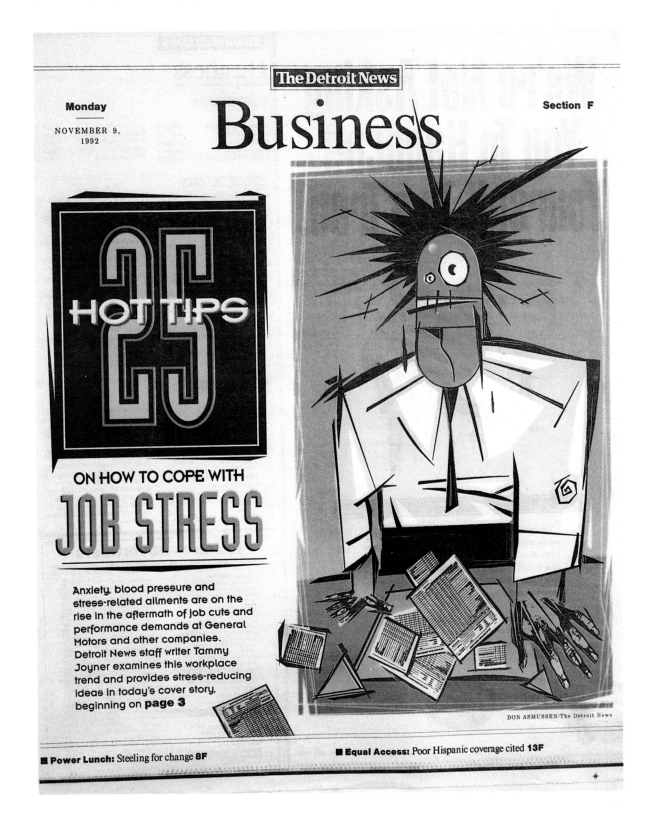

Silver

The Miami Herald

Ana Lense-Larrauri, Designer/Illustrator; Jim Watters,
Business Monday News Editor; Rex Seline, Executive
Business Editor; Randy Stano, Director/Editorial Art &
Design

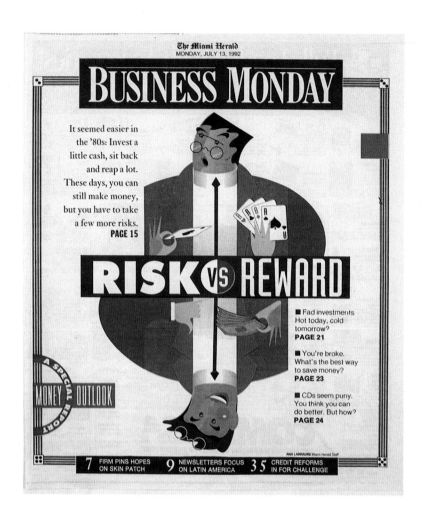

Award of Excellence

American Medical News

Chicago, IL

Barbara Dow, Art Director & Designer; Elizabeth Lada, Illustrator

Award of Excellence

Asbury Park Press

Neptune, NJ

Mark Kseniak, Page Designer; Sean McNaughton,
Graphics Artist; Peter Ackerman, Photographer; Andrew
Prendimano, Art Director

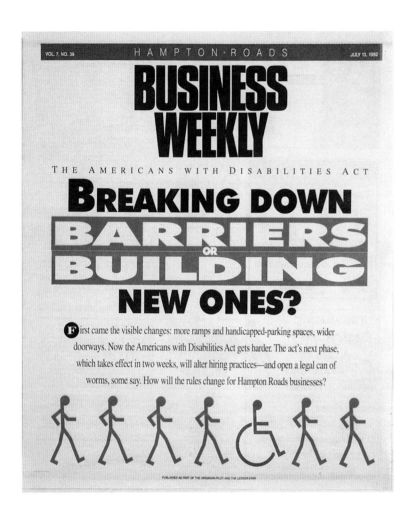

Silver

The Virginian-Pilot

Norfolk, VA

Jeff Glick, Art Director; Bob Fleming, Editor

Award of Excellence

The Atlanta Journal/Constitution

Tony De Feria, Art Director & Designer; Mike Gordon, Design Director; Charles Haddad, Writer; Caesar Williams, Editor; Chuck Eckstein, Editor

Award of Excellence

The Columbus Dispatch

Columbus, OH

Roderick Harris, Designer; Scott Minister, Art Director

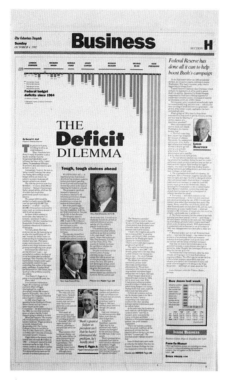

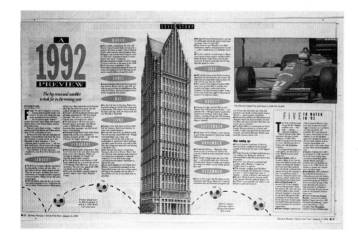

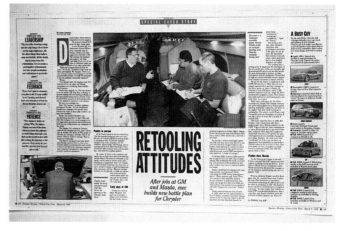

Award of Excellence

The Detroit News

Sid Jablonski, Artist; David Pierce, Artist; Michele Fecht, Researcher; Felix Grabowski, Graphics

Award of Excellence

Detroit Free Press

Steve Anderson, Art Director & Designer; David Cowles, Illustrator

Award of Excellence

The Detroit News

Don Asmussen, Artist & Designer; Felix Grabowski, Art Director

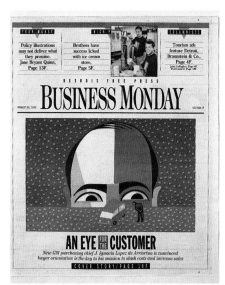

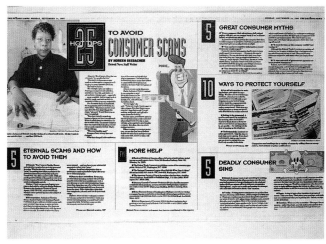

Award of Excellence

Los Angeles Times

James Owens, Designer & Illustrator; Vicky McCargar, Graphics Coordinator

Award of Excellence

Los Angeles Times

James Owens, Designer & Illustrator; Vicky McCargar, Graphics Coordinator

Award of Excellence

The Miami Herald

Ana Lense-Larrauri, Designer & Illustrator; Jim Watters, Business Monday News Editor; Rex Seline, Executive Business Editor; Randy Stano, Director/Editorial Art & Design

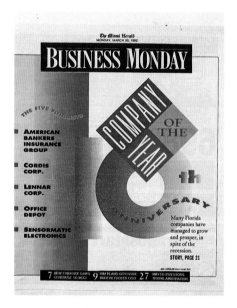

Award of Excellence

The Miami Herald

Ana Lense-Larrauri, Designer & Illustrator; Jim Watters, Business Monday News Editor; Rex Seline, Executive Business Editor; Randy Stano, Director/Editorial Art & Design

Award of Excellence

The Miami Herald

Ana Lense-Larrauri, Designer & Illustrator; Jim Watters, Business Monday News Editor; Rex Seline, Executive Business Editor; Randy Stano, Director/Editorial Art & Design

Award of Excellence

The Miami Herald

Ana Lense-Larrauri, Designer & Illustrator; Jim Watters, Business Monday News Editor; Rex Seline, Executive Business Editor; Randy Stano, Director/Editorial Art & Design

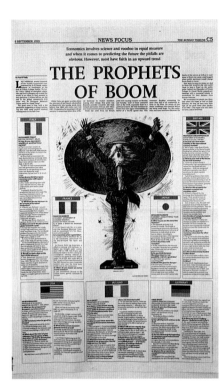

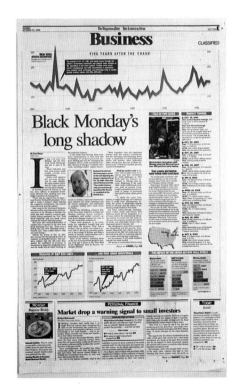

Silver

Detroit Free Press

Wayne Kamidoi, Designer

Detroit Free Press
Sports
WEEKEND

KA-BOOM

Ted Jayson fires his classic muzzle loader. Other aficionados prefer updated weapons. Page 7F.

COLLEGE BASKETBALL
- MSU guard hopes to make point, Page 2F

NFL
- Week 15 matchups, TV games, Page 4F

ALSO INSIDE
- Weekend TV, Page 2F
- Preps, Page 6F
- Scoreboard, Page 9F

Friday, Dec. 11, 1992 Section F

Scores: 1-900-370-0990 (75 cents per call). Sports: 222-6660

Rodman's life on the rebound

MITCH ALBOM

There was a knock on the door. Dennis Rodman, who was not answering knocks or phones, peeked out the window. He did not recognize the man, or the little boy, or the pickup truck.

He cracked the door open.

"This is from the Pistons," the man said, holding out an envelope. Rodman took it. Inside was a neatly typed notice saying he had been suspended, without pay, effective immediately. After six years of a storybook NBA career, he was off the team. Rodman stared at the paper.

"Uh, Dennis?" the delivery man said.

"Huh?"

"This is my son. Can he have your autograph?"

What do you do when your world is a contradiction?

When your bosses want you, but your bosses suspend you? When people ask for your autograph, then whisper that you're crazy? When the daughter you love can't be with you, can't even see you, and, in grief, you tattoo her face on your forearm and make a Christmas video showing presents you will mail to her?

To understand Dennis Rodman — to even understand a story about him — you must unhook your standard gauges, because he has been living in this very strange place, and is only now surfacing from its cold waters. Hold him up to normal rules, he shrivels. Judge him by the real world, he seems spoiled and pampered.

Sure, most Americans don't get paid time off to think about their lives. And they can't use divorce or depression

as a reason for skipping work. But such logic will get you no closer to unlocking the enigma of Dennis Rodman.

To do that, you must talk to him, really talk to him, and listen to his riddled responses. Inside that rubber-band body — which houses the greatest rebounder in basketball today — there also lives a little boy, a millionaire, a tractor driver and an American celebrity.

All trying to make peace with one another.

"It wasn't just my marriage breaking up that killed me," says Rodman, 31, standing alone after a practice this week. "It was everything happening at once. My daughter. Chuck Daly leaving. John Salley leaving. It was

See MITCH ALBOM, Page 6F

Browns' Kosar at top of his, uh, form

BY MICHELLE KAUFMAN
Free Press Sports Writer

CLEVELAND — A woman once approached Bernie Kosar during a golf outing and offered to help him with his peculiar swing.

"You've got to follow through like you do with your overhand pass," she suggested.

Kosar, who has a 9-handicap, smiled and replied, "Ma'am, you must not follow pro football very closely."

Bernie Kosar

If she did, she would have known that Kosar's passes are anything but conventional. The 6-foot-5, gangly quarterback is admittedly about as graceful as a Manute Bol in five-inch pumps. He probably has thrown as many passes underhand as overhand, and hundreds more somewhere around elbow level.

But Kosar's lack of style is welcome in the Cleveland Browns' locker room. It doesn't matter that he throws incorrectly, so long as he throws completions. His teammates are glad to have him back after seeing him on the sidelines nine games with a broken ankle.

"I've seen him flip a pass with two hands, I've seen him toss it underhand like a basketball, I've seen him throw it every which way," said halfback Eric Metcalf. "As long as it gets to the receiver, that's all that counts. Who wants to look pretty and be 0-of-30?"

Quarterback coach Gary Tranquill, who has been in the business 30 years, was stunned when he first saw Kosar.

"Before I got here, I had never seen anyone as mechanically deficient, and that's putting it mildly," Tranquill said. "But if you watch him closely, for what he does, he does it well. You just don't change a guy like that."

Said receiver Lawyer Tillman: "He

See KOSAR, Page 2F

A SKI MECCA

Skiers flock to Petoskey's Boyne resorts, Nubs Nob

BY WYLIE GERDES
Free Press Sports Writer

WEEKEND WATCH

Harbor Springs dentist Bill Zoerhof has an apt characterization of his old stomping grounds in northwest Lower Michigan: "For 10 Saturdays a winter, it's as wild as any place in the country."

Zoerhof — an amateur guitarist and bandleader — was describing the Zoo bar at Boyne Highlands, but he could have been picturing the ski season in the Petoskey area. Beginning with Christmas week, the Petoskey-Harbor Springs area is inundated with a flood of skiers that makes it the capital of Michigan skiing.

The area is blessed with three major ski hills — the sister areas of Boyne Mountain and Boyne Highlands, and Nubs Nob. Among them, they sell around 400,000 lift tickets a season. On the busiest weekends, nearly 15,000 skiers will pack an area of about 24,000 full-time residents.

The big draw is the concentration of three distinctly different ski areas. Boyne Highlands, the everything for everybody area, is almost directly across M-119 from Nubs Nob, the locals' favorite. About 20 miles away is

See PETOSKEY, Page 7F

JIM SZABO/Special to the Free Press

Wings meet on winter of discontent

Most deny conspiracy theory against coach

BY KEITH GAVE
Free Press Sports Writer

That double-barreled shotgun the Red Wings seem to have pointed at Bryan Murray might be loaded with blanks.

Their uninspired play in losses this week to their two biggest rivals begs the question: Are they playing to have the coach fired?

"Yes," one veteran player said bluntly after their 5-3 loss Wednesday night at Toronto. "That's a ridiculous question," said another after Thursday's practice, which included a soul-searching two-hour-long meeting with Murray.

And captain Steve Yzerman had this conclusion: "He's the general manager, too, so he swings a lot of weight. I think the players will go before the coach does."

Meanwhile, Murray was trying to arrange a trade to help improve his team instead of fretting for his job.

Besides, he revealed Thursday that he agreed to terms on a new contract two weeks ago. "It's a done deal," he said, refusing to discuss terms of the agreement.

The Wings take a 1-6-1 skid into tonight's game against Philadelphia at Joe Louis Arena. In that span, they have fallen from first in the Norris

See RED WINGS, Page 3F

EXPANDING

The NHL Board of Governors awarded expansion franchises to South Florida and Orange County, Calif., beginning either next season or in 1994-95. The California team might play in the new Anaheim Arena. The South Florida team likely will play at least initially in Miami Arena. NHL Roundup, Page 3F.

It's just another day on the slopes. Above, Kim Fox of Traverse City and Clarke Hare of Cass City arrive at Boyne Mountain. At left, Mike and Diane George of Grand Rapids pack up after a day at Boyne.

Tigers lose Tanana to Mets, sign veteran lefty Bolton

BY JOHN LOWE
Free Press Sports Writer

Frank Tanana joined the New York Mets Thursday because the Tigers thought he was too old.

Tanana, a 39-year-old free-agent left-hander, signed a one-year deal with New York after the Tigers didn't offer him a contract. The Mets guaranteed $1.5 million, with incentives that can make the deal worth the same $1.7 million he made last season.

"I'm extremely surprised the Tigers didn't offer me a contract," said Tanana, whose first choice was to remain in Detroit, where he was born and lives. "I wouldn't have been surprised if I'd had a poor year. But we

See TIGERS, Page 3F

- Key signs for $17 million with Yankees. Nation/World, Page 2F.

finished sixth, and I won 13 games."

"It hurts not to keep Frank," said general manager Jerry Walker. "Frank is a tremendous guy and has done a lot for the club."

Walker signed a free-agent left-hander Thursday: Tom Bolton, 30, who spent last season with Boston and Cincinnati. The Tigers envision him as a starter and reliever — the swing role that Les Lancaster couldn't fill last season. If Bolton is successful, his price ($400,000 for one year) is a bargain.

ALL 92 METRO
FREE PRESS

THE BEST PLAYERS IN TOWN? Meet the Free Press' All-Metro team: Plymouth Canton's Stephanie Gray, who will score from inside and out for Western Michigan; Grosse Pointe South's Angela Drake, who has played only four years but gets four more at Toledo; Rochester Adams' Jeannine Augustin, a lightning-quick terror signed by Notre Dame; Harper Woods Regina's Paula Sanders, the Miss Basketball runner-up bound for MSU; and Birmingham Marian's Stephanie Storen, who won the state title. Marian's Mary Lillie-Cicerone is the coach. Story, Page 6F.

Award of Excellence

Anchorage Daily News

Mike Campbell, AME; William Dawson, Page Designer

Award of Excellence

Asbury Park Press

Neptune, NJ

Tim Oliver, Page Designer; Peter Ackerman, Photographer

Award of Excellence

Asbury Park Press

Neptune, NJ

Harris Siegel, Page Designer; James J. Connolly, Photographer; Thomas P. Costello, Photographer; Joe Sullivan, Editor

Award of Excellence

Asbury Park Press

Neptune, NJ

Harris Siegel, Page Designer; Stacey Martin, Graphic Artist; Mike Donofrio, Editor

Award of Excellence

Asbury Park Press

Neptune, NJ

Harris Siegel, Page Designer

Award of Excellence

Asbury Park Press

Neptune, NJ

Harris Siegel, Page Designer; James J Connolly, Photographer; Joe Sullivan, Editor

Award of Excellence

The Detroit News

Dierck Casselman, AME Graphics/Design; Michael
Green, Photographer

Award of Excellence

The Detroit News

Sports Staff

Award of Excellence

El Norte

Monterrey, Mexico

Perla Olmeda Cepeda, Designer; Bill Hickey, Allsport
Photographer; Doug Pensinger, Allsport Photographer

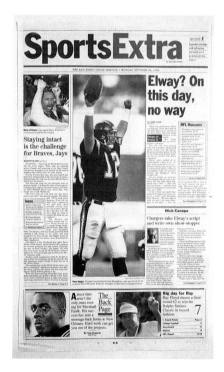

Award of Excellence

The Miami Herald

Phill Flanders, Illustrator; Bill Grant, Sports Design
Editor; Randy Stano, Director/Editorial Art & Design

Award of Excellence

The Miami Herald

Phil Flanders, Illustrator; Bill Grant, Sports Design
Editor; Randy Stano, Director/Editorial Art & Design

Award of Excellence

The San Diego Union-Tribune

Stan McNeal, Designer

Award of Excellence
The Wichita Eagle
Wichita, KS
Randy Stephenson, Staff Artist

Award of Excellence
The Citizen
Auburn, NY
Gary Piccirillo, AME Design

Award of Excellence
Stavanger Aftenblad
Stavanger, Norway
Gottfred Tunge, Copy Editor

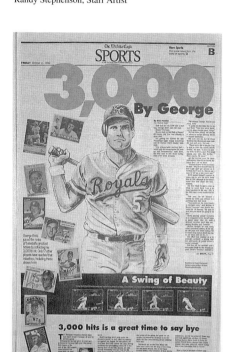

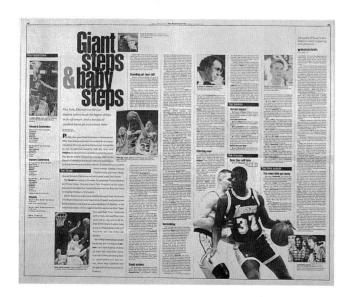

Award of Excellence
San Jose Mercury News
Albert Poon, Designer; Sam Hundley, Features Design Director; David Tepps,
Deputy Executive Sports Editor; Mike Guersch, Copy Editor

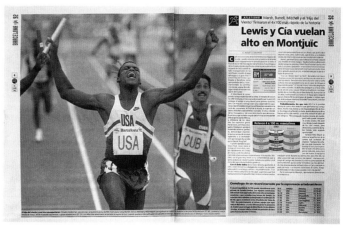

Award of Excellence
El Mundo Deportivo
Barcelona, Spain
Graphics & Design Departments

Gold

The Atlanta Journal/Constitution

Peter Dishal, Designer/Illustrator; Mike Gordon, Design Director; Tony De Feria, Art Director; Glenn Hannigan, Editor

SECTION D

Barcelona Olympics

THE ATLANTA JOURNAL
THE ATLANTA CONSTITUTION

Tuesday, July 28, 1992

INSIDE

Pablo's masterpiece

Knight Ridder Tribune

Morales's race for gold highlights day for U.S. swimmers

For three years, he was retired. Three years. That's how devastated **Pablo Morales** (above) was after failing to make the 1988 Olympic team; he had scored two silver medals in '84. His mother's death from cancer last year partly triggered a comeback. And when he bobbed out of the water, winner of the 100-meter butterfly Monday (Story, page D4), Morales pointed to his father, who sat in the stands with a picture of his late wife. Morales was part of a mixed day for U.S. swimmers. **Doug Gjertsen** of Dunwoody (right) wore a Braves cap on the medal stand after swimming the anchor leg of the 800-meter freestyle relay. The U.S. foursome was a disappointing third. **Nicole Haislett** won the 200 freestyle in a final that shockingly excluded gold-medal candidate **Jenny Thompson,** who "choked bigtime" and failed to qualify. **Anita Nall,** favored in the 200 breaststroke, faded to third. Today, two other old-timers try to pick up on Morales's momentum as **Janet Evans** and **Matt Biondi** hunt for gold. (Story, page D2)

MARLENE KARAS/Staff

No upset here: U.S. humbles Croatia

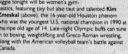

Associated Press

Upset? What upset? Croatia, given the best chance of anyone to ambush the U.S. men's basketball team, went meekly 103-70 (Story, page D3). There was an upset player — yes, him, **Charles Barkley** — and a potentially upsetting injury to **Magic Johnson** (left). He limped off with a knee injury midway through the first half and did not return. He may miss two games, including Germany on Wednesday. And Barkley, the ambassador of bad will, added more antics to his flagrant elbow against Angola on Sunday. He angrily slammed the ball to the floor, cursed a fan and drew another technical. And how easy will the U.S. have it Wednesday? Angola, which lost to the Dream Team by 68, scared the daylights out of Germany Monday, falling by a point. Rest that knee, Magic. As long as you need.

TODAY ON TV

They're tanned, taut and talented, and tonight's the night to catch their act. World champion **Kent Ferguson** leads America's divers in the quest for gold, hoping to make up for his failure to win a spot on the 1984 and 1988 U.S. Olympic teams. Check out our coverage on Page D2. The other TV biggie tonight will be women's gymnastics, featuring tiny but also taut and talented **Kim Zmeskal** (above), the 16-year-old Houston phenom who was the youngest U.S. national champion in 1990 at the ripe old age of 14. Late-night Olympic buffs can tune in to boxing, weightlifting and Greco-Roman wrestling, along with the American volleyball team's battle against Canada.

EN BARCELONA

It's not Hemingway's Paris or Woody Allen's Manhattan, but a certain magic lingers nonetheless over Barcelona's night streets. The favored spot for a leisurely evening stroll is Las Ramblas, where broad-leafed hardwoods line the way and lovers of all ages huddle on benches. As midnight draws near, the street teems with nightlife — bars, restaurants and a never-ending stretch of sidewalk cafes where dark Latin men and raven-haired women stir coffee, stare at passers-by, or lean in close for intimate conversation. But if Las Ramblas holds the city's heart, Avenida Reina Maria Cristina has captured its spirit. Stretching but 250 yards, the street sweeps from Placa d'Espanya to the base of Montjuic, a small mountain that is site of many of the events. Its entire length is lined with powerful fountains, a colonnade of 20-foot geysers that walk the tourist's eye up the incline. Crowning the scene is the National Museum of Art, perched on the mountain's crest.

ON THE SCENE

Bob Dart, normally an Atlanta Journal-Constitution Washington correspondent, is delighted to be in Barcelona instead of chasing presidential candidates around America. He's already accomplished his most important assignment — buying official Olympics T-shirts for his kids — and will continue to chronicle the people and peripheries of the Games. Dart lived in Atlanta and wrote about the South for the Journal and Constitution for seven years before joining the Washington Bureau in 1983. The fact he's here shows he's learned a bit about lobbying.

Bronze

Chicago Tribune

Stephen Ravenscraft, Art
Director; Tony Majeri, Senior
Design Director; Stephen
Cvengros, Editor

Award of Excellence

The Atlanta Journal/Constitution

Peter Dishal, Designer; Mike Gordon, Design Director;
Tony De Feria, Art Director; Glenn Hannagan, Editor

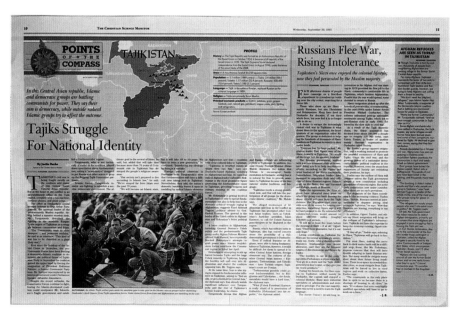

Bronze

The Christian Science Monitor

Shirley Horn, Graphics Artist; Marianne Le Pelley,
Picture Editor; Karen Everbeck, Page Designer

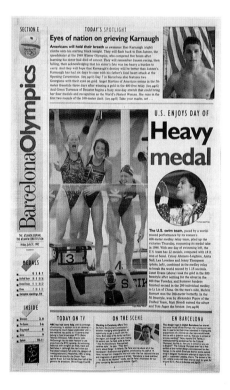

Award of Excellence

The Atlanta Journal/Constitution

Robert Mashburn, Designer/Illustrator; Mike Gordon,
Design Director; Tony De Feria, Art Director; Glenn
Hannigan, Editor

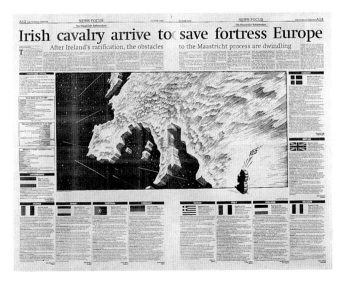

Award of Excellence
The Orange County Register

Santa Ana, CA

Brenda Shoun, Assistant News Editor/Design; Nam Nguyen, Graphics Artist; Stephen Rountree, Graphics Artist; George Turney, Graphics Artist; Tom Ward, Graphics Artist; Chas Metivier, Photographer; Venetia Lai, News Editor/Visuals (Graphics); Kevin Byrne, News Editor/Design; Nanette Bisher, AME & Art Director; Gary Robbins, Reporter

Award of Excellence
The Orange County Register
Santa Ana, CA

Tom Ward, Illustrator; David Medzerian, Assistant News Editor/Design; Venetia Lai, News Editor/Visuals (Graphics)

Award of Excellence
The Orange County Register
Santa Ana, CA

Karen Kelso, Assistant News Editor/Design; George Turney, Graphics Artist

Award of Excellence
San Francisco Chronicle

Hulda Nelson, Art Director; Steve Outing, Graphics Editor; Steve Kearsley, Designer; Bruce Krefting, Map Designer; Alyx Metzler, Researcher; Kris Strawser, Graphics Artist; John Boring, Graphics Artist; Bill Smith, Graphics Artist; Lourdes Livingston, Graphics Artist

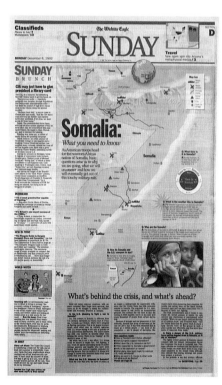

Award of Excellence
The Sunday Tribune
Dublin, Ireland

Stephen Ryan, Design Editor & Designer; Paul Hipkins, Production Editor; John Carlos, Photographer

Award of Excellence
The Wichita Eagle
Wichita, KS

Jeff Pulaski, Staff Artist; Paul Soutar, Graphics Director; Bill Baker, KRT Artist; Ron Coddington, KRT Artist

The UCSD Guardian

La Jolla, CA

James Collier, Designer/Design Editor; Mel Marcelo, Artist/Graphics Editor

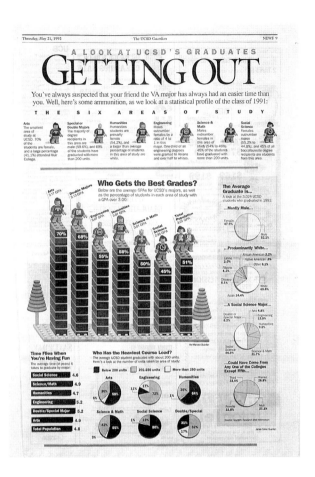

Award of Excellence

The Times-Picayune

New Orleans, LA

George Berke, Design Director; Kurt Mutchler, Graphics Editor; Michael Jantze, Assistant Graphics Editor

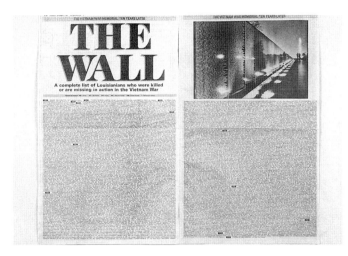

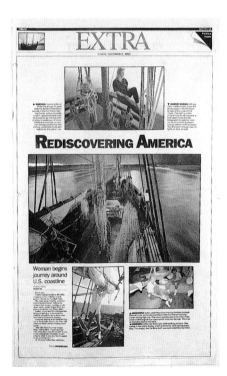

Award of Excellence

Stavanger Aftenblad

Stavanger, Norway

Einar Risa, Sub Editor

Award of Excellence

News-Press

Fort Myers, FL

Randy Lovely, AME/Design; Paul Fresty, Graphics Editor; Cathy Riddick, Special Projects Editor

Award of Excellence

The Tribune

Fort Pierce, FL

Wade Wilson, News Editor; William Ide, Photographer

Award of Excellence

The Florida Times-Union

Jacksonville, FL

D. Tom Patterson, AME Graphics

Award of Excellence

The Sun-Sentinel

Ft. Lauderdale, FL

Staff

Award of Excellence

The Detroit News

Dale Peskin, AME; Joe Gray, Assistant News Editor;
Felecia Henderson, Copy Editor & Designer

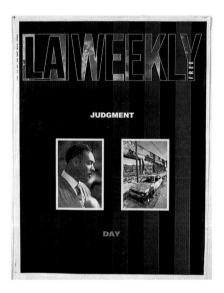

Award of Excellence

The Times-Picayune

New Orleans, LA

Kurt Mutchler, Graphics Editor; Tom Gregory, News Associate Editor; Doug
Parker, Assistant Photo Editor; Dinah Rogers, Assistant Photo Editor; Staff

Award of Excellence

L.A. Weekly

Los Angeles, CA

Scott Ford, Art Director; William Smith, Associate Art
Director; Ted Soqui, Photographer; Cynthia Wiggins,
Photographer; Virginia Lee Hunter, Photographer;
Larry Hirshowitz, Photographer; Debra DiPaolo,
Photographer

Silver

The New York Times

Peter Putrimas, Makeup Editor; Jim Mones, Makeup Editor; Lee Frempong, Makeup Editor; Al Granberg, Maps Artist; John Papasian, Maps Artist; Tom Bodkin, Design Director

Silver

Barcelona '92

Pamplona, Spain

Ricardo Bermejo, Art Director & Designer (BEGA); Luis Garbayo, News Editor/Designer (BEGA); Guillermo Nagore, Design Editor; Rafa Esquiroz, Designer (BEGA)

■ La emoción invadió anoche a los asistentes a la ceremonia de inauguración de los Juegos Olímpicos y a los 3.500 millones de telespectadores que la siguieron en todo el mundo. La expresividad artística del espectáculo y la solemnidad fueron las notas dominantes de una noche mágica consagrada a la imaginación y al ritual olímpico. Barcelona entera se conmovió en el momento en que el Rey Juan Carlos declaró inaugurados los Juegos de XXV Olimpíada; un sueño largamente perseguido se hizo realidad y la ciudad desbordó de alegría. Bravo por los Juegos.

■ L'émotion a envahi hier soir, les spectateurs de la cérémonie d'ouverture des Jeux Olympiques et les 3,5 milliards de téléspectateurs qui l'ont suivie dans le monde entier. L'aspect artistique du spectacle et la solennité ont été les traits caractéristiques de cette nuit magique dédiée à l'imagination et au rituel olympique. Tout Barcelone a été ému au moment où le Roi Juan Carlos a déclaré les Jeux de la XXVème olympiade ouverts; un rêve très longtemps poursuivi est devenu réalité et la ville a débordé de joie. Bravo pour les Jeux!

Award of Excellence
Diario 16
Madrid, Spain
Carlos Perez Diaz, Art Director & Designer; Staff

Award of Excellence
Barcelona '92
Pamplona, Spain
Ricardo Bermejo, Art Director (BEGA); Luis Garbayo, News Editor/Design (BEGA); Guillermo Nagore, Design Editor; Rafa Esquiroz, Designer (BEGA); Layout Staff

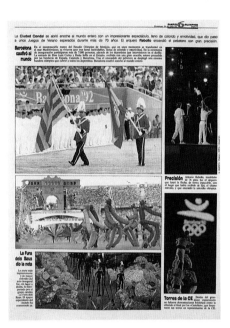

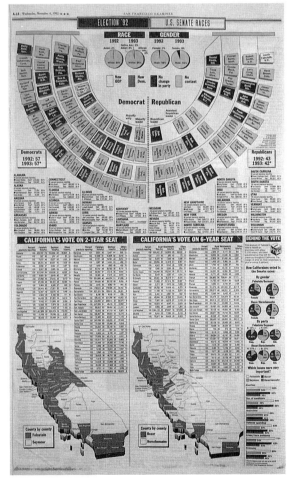

Bronze
San Francisco Examiner
Kelly Frankeny, Art Director; Bob McLeod, Photo Director; Staff

Award of Excellence

Detroit Free Press

Deborah Withey, Design Director; Lee Yarosh, Designer; Wayne Kamidoi, Designer; Ken McDonald, Designer; Sue Parker, Designer; James Denk, Designer; Keith Webb, Designer

Award of Excellence

The Detroit News

Dale Peskin, AME; Nancy Hanus, Assistant News Editor

Award of Excellence

The Orange County Register

Santa Ana, CA

Staff

Award of Excellence

Diario 16

Madrid, Spain

Carlos Perez Diaz, Art Director & Designer; Javier Jimenez, Designer

Award of Excellence

El Norte

Monterrey, Mexico

Ileana Gorostleta, Designer

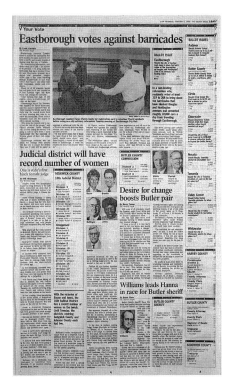

Award of Excellence
The Wichita Eagle

Wichita, KS

Alice Sky, News Editor/Visuals; Tim Potter, Page Designer; Jeff Rush, Page
Designer; Richard Crowson, Editorial Cartoonist; Jeff Pulaski, Staff Artist;
Paul Soutar, Graphics Director; Photo Staff

Silver

The Detroit News

Dale Peskin, AME; Dierck Casselman, AME; Sports Staff

Silver

The Detroit News

Dale Peskin, AME; Nancy Hanus, Assistant News Editor; Joe Gray, Assistant News Editor

Bronze

The Times-Picayune

New Orleans, LA

George Berke, Design Director; Kurt Mutchler, Graphics Editor; Billy Turner, Assistant Sports Editor; Doug Parker, Assistant Photo Editor; Dinah Rogers, Assistant Photo Editor

Award of Excellence

Chicago Tribune

Steve Little, Graphic Artist; Stephen Ravenscraft, Graphic Artist; Don Sena, Graphic Coordinator; Terry Volpp, Assistant Graphics Editor; Vasin Omer D., Graphic Artist; Tracy Herman, Graphic Coordinator; Rick Tuma, Graphic Artist; Nancy I.Z. Reese, Associate Graphics Editor; Martin Fischer, Graphic Coordinator; David Jahntz, Graphic Artist

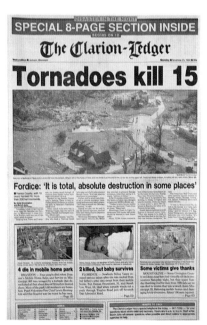

Award of Excellence

The Clarion-Ledger

Jackson, MS

Staff

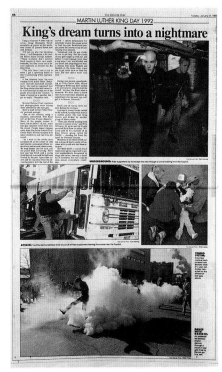

Award of Excellence
The Denver Post

Jim Bates, Executive News Editor; Steve Larson, Photo
Editor; John Epperson, Photographer; Karl Gehring,
Photographer; Jerry Cleveland, Photographer; Kent Meireis,
Photographer; John Sunderland, Photographer; Leslie
Jorgensen, Artist

Award of Excellence

Los Angeles Daily News

Woodland Hills, CA

Staff

Award of Excellence

The New York Times

Tom Bodkin, Design Director; Margaret O'Connor, Deputy Design Director; Brent Hatcher, Graphics Editor; Jim Mones, Makeup Editor; Jack Pfeifer, Makeup Editor; Jim Perry, Map Artist

Award of Excellence

The News-Sentinel

Fort Wayne, IN

Dan Suwyn, Design Director; Tom Bissett, Designer; Cindy Jones-Hulfachor, Graphics Reporter; Denise Reagan, Graphics Reporter; Brian Tombaugh, Photographer

Award of Excellence

Portland Press Herald

Portland, ME

Bob Dixon, Copy Desk Chief; Andrea Philbrick, Design Editor; Ken Jones, Designer; Sandra Shriver, Photo Editor; Mike McGee, Designer; John Ewing, Photographer

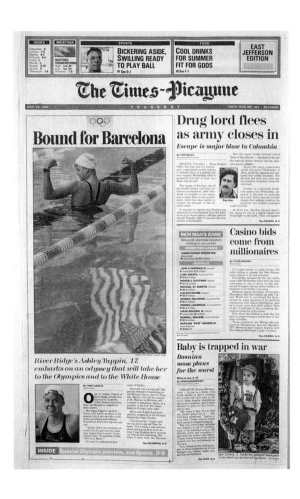

Award of Excellence

The Times-Picayune

New Orleans, LA

George Berke, Design Director; Kurt Mutchler,
Graphics Editor; Ray Lincoln, News Editor; Doug
Parker, Assistant Photo Editor

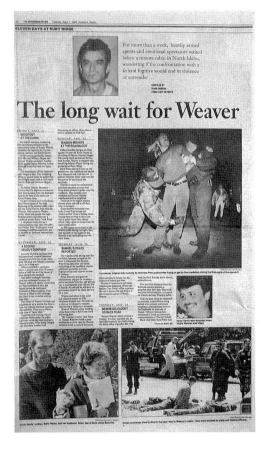

Award of Excellence

The Spokesman-Review

Spokane, WA

Scott Sines, AME/Visual; Neal Pattison, AME; John Kafentzis, News Editor; Kevin Graman,
Assistant News Editor; Vince Grippi, Graphics Editor; Photo Staff

Silver

The New York Times

Fred Norgaard, Art Director; Joe Ward, Graphics Editor; John Papasian, Graphics; Seth Feaster, Graphics; Bedel Saget, Graphics; Neil Amdur, Sports Editor; Sandy Bailey, Deputy Sports Editor; Rich Rosenbush, Makeup Editor; Tom Bodkin, Design Director

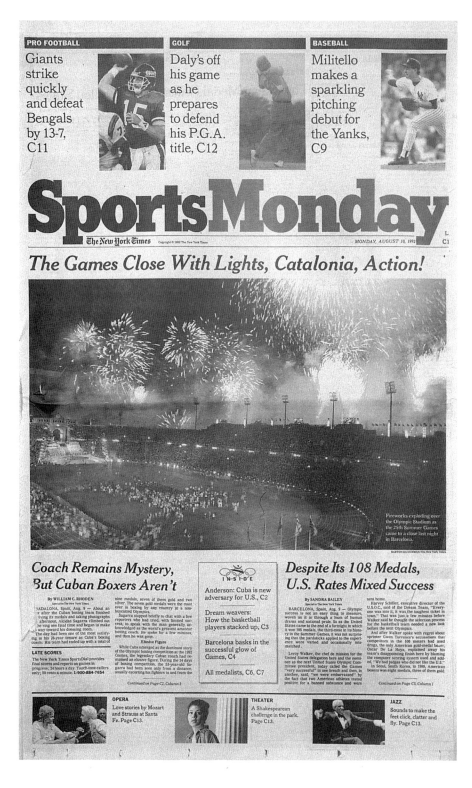

PRO FOOTBALL
Giants strike quickly and defeat Bengals by 13-7, C11

GOLF
Daly's off his game as he prepares to defend his P.G.A. title, C12

BASEBALL
Militello makes a sparkling pitching debut for the Yanks, C9

SportsMonday

The New York Times — Copyright © 1992 The New York Times — MONDAY, AUGUST 10, 1992 — L C1

The Games Close With Lights, Catalonia, Action!

Fireworks exploding over the Olympic Stadium as the 25th Summer Games came to a close last night in Barcelona.

BARTON SILVERMAN/The New York Times

Coach Remains Mystery, But Cuban Boxers Aren't

By WILLIAM C. RHODEN
Special to The New York Times

BADALONA, Spain, Aug. 9 — About an hour after the Cuban boxing team finished driving its medals and taking photographs this afternoon, Alcidas Sagarra climbed out of the ring one final time and began to make his way toward his dressing room.

The day had been one of the most satisfying in his 28-year tenure as Cuba's boxing coach: His team had ended up with a total of nine medals, seven of them gold and two silver. The seven gold medals were the most ever in boxing by any country in a non-boycotted Olympics.

Sagarra stopped briefly to chat with a few reporters who had tried, with limited success, to speak with the man generally acknowledged as the world's greatest amateur boxing coach. He spoke for a few minutes, and then he was gone.

Elusive Figure

While Cuba emerged as the dominant story of the Olympic boxing competition at the 1992 Games, the legendary Cuban coach had remained an elusive figure. During the 14 days of boxing competition, the 53-year-old Sagarra had been seen only from a distance, usually exporting his fighters to and from the

LATE SCORES
The New York Times SportsDial provides final scores and reports on games in progress; 24 hours a day. Touch-tone callers only; 50 cents a minute. 1-900-884-7654

Continued on Page C2, Column 3

INSIDE
Anderson: Cuba is new adversary for U.S., C2

Dream weavers: How the basketball players stacked up, C3

Barcelona basks in the successful glow of Games, C4

All medalists, C6, C7

Despite Its 108 Medals, U.S. Rates Mixed Success

By SANDRA BAILEY
Special to The New York Times

BARCELONA, Spain, Aug. 9 — Olympic success is not an easy thing to measure, woven as it is through a skein of human drama and national pride. So as the United States came to the end of a fortnight in which it won 108 medals, the third-most in history in the Summer Games, it was not surprising that the yardsticks applied to performance were varied and occasionally mismatched.

Leroy Walker, the chef de mission for the United States delegation here and the nominee as the next United States Olympic Committee president, today called the Games "very successful" in one breath and then, in another, said, "we were embarrassed" by the fact that two American athletes tested positive for a banned substance and were sent home.

Harvey Schiller, executive director of the U.S.O.C., said of the Dream Team, "Everyone was into it, it was the toughest ticket in town." That was just a few minutes before Walker said he thought the selection process for the basketball team needed a new look before the next Olympics.

And after Walker spoke with regret about sprinter Gwen Torrence's accusations that competitors in the 100 meters had used drugs, the only American gold-medal boxer, Oscar De La Hoya, explained away his team's disappointing finish here by blaming the computer scoring system used and added, "We had judges who did not like the U.S."

In Seoul, South Korea, in 1988, Americans boxers won eight medals, three of them gold.

Continued on Page C3, Column 1

OPERA Love stories by Mozart and Strauss at Santa Fe. Page C13.

THEATER A Shakespearean challenge in the park. Page C13.

JAZZ Sounds to make the feet click, clatter and fly. Page C13.

Novice Is Foiled By Loose Goggles

12 Angry (Bald) Men Set Out to Make Point

Unlikely Olympic Marathon for Becker

No Politics, Just Power For the Pocket Hercules

Special TripleCast Values!
1 DAY—NOW JUST $19.95
WEEKEND RATE—$39.95 (Saturday & Sunday)

Bronze

El Pais

Madrid, Spain

J. Ignacio Tamargo, Designer; Javier Lopez, Art Director

EL PAIS
Olímpico
DIARIO DE LOS JUEGOS DE BARCELONA   7 DE AGOSTO DE 1992 / NÚMERO 14

▲ El estadounidense Young celebra por los suelos su magnífico triunfo en 400 metros vallas.

RICARDO GUTIÉRREZ

Atletismo de bandera

Young bate el récord de Moses; Peñalver logra plata en decatlón; Lewis suma su séptimo oro

SUMARIO

13 — Estados Unidos y Croacia, final del torneo de baloncesto

19 — Arrese y el doble femenino lucharán por la medalla de oro

14 — La técnica, una alternativa a los estimulantes

▲ Arantxa y Conchita celebran su triunfo de ayer.

RESULTADOS Página 22   TELEVISIÓN Página 27

EL PAIS
Olímpico
DIARIO DE LOS JUEGOS DE BARCELONA   8 DE AGOSTO DE 1992 / NÚMERO 15

SUMARIO

9 — El hockey sobre hierba femenino gana para España el primer oro en deportes de equipo

▲ La española Teresa Motos avanza entre la defensa alemana.

Marín, noveno en 50 kilómetros marcha, a los 42 años de edad

Peñalver: "En el decatlón nos ayudamos entre todos. Es la mutua misericordia"

9-18 — España aspira hoy a mejorar su medallero con fútbol, tenis, waterpolo y atletismo

10 — Jennifer Capriati desbanca a Steffi Graf

RESULTADOS Página 19   TELEVISIÓN Página 27

▲ Serguéi Bubka cae hacia la lona sin haber superado el listón.

ANTONIO ESPEJO

Bubka fracasa en su hora clave

El desastre del favorito indiscutible permitió que García Chico lograse el bronce en pértiga

La agonía parte de Mataró y dura 42.195 metros

Primero el trote, después Zatopek y por fin Abebe Bikila

Itinerario del maratón (42,195km)

THE BEST OF NEWSPAPER DESIGN **75**

Award of Excellence

Detroit Free Press

Tracee Hamilton, Designer; Tom Panzenhagen, Designer

Award of Excellence

San Jose Mercury News

Geri Migielicz, Photography Director; Sue Morrow, Graphics Editor; Jim Gensheimer, Photographer

Award of Excellence

Barcelona '92

Pamplona, Spain

Ricardo Bermejo, Art Director & Designer (BEGA); Luis Garbayo, News Editor/Design (BEGA); Guillermo Nagore, Design Editor; Rafa Esquiroz, Designer (BEGA); Juancho Cruz, Layout Staff; Eduardo Cruz, Layout Staff; Pablo Lopez, Layout Staff; Fernando Lopez Urdin, Layout Staff; Roser de Manuel-Rimbau, Layout Staff; Anna Nogue, Layout Staff

Award of Excellence

Barcelona '92

Pamplona, Spain

Ricardo Bermejo, Art Director & Designer (BEGA); Luis Garbayo, News Editor/Design (BEGA); Guillermo Nagore, Design Editor; Rafa Esquiroz, Designer (BEGA); Juancho Cruz, Infographics; Pablo Lopez, Cover Artist; Fernando Lopez Urdin, Photo Editor; Eduardo Cruz, Layout Staff; Roser de Manuel-Rimbau, Layout Staff; Anna Nogue, Layout Staff

Award of Excellence

El Mundo Deportivo

Barcelona, Spain

Staff Graphics & Design Departments

Award of Excellence

The Albuquerque Tribune

Mike Davis, Photo Editor; Mike Gallegos, Photo Editor;
David Carrillo, Designer; Annemarie Neff, Designer;
David Carlson, Designer; Lara Edge, Designer; Karlan
Massey, Designer; Jeff Neumann, Graphics Artist;
Charlotte Hill, Graphics Artist; Randall K. Roberts,
AME Graphics

Award of Excellence

The Wall Street Journal

James Condon, Graphics Director; Marco Herrera,
Designer; Dan Ion, Graphic Artist; Germaine Keller,
Graphic Artist; Michele Shapiro, Typesetting

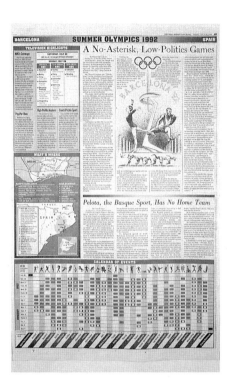

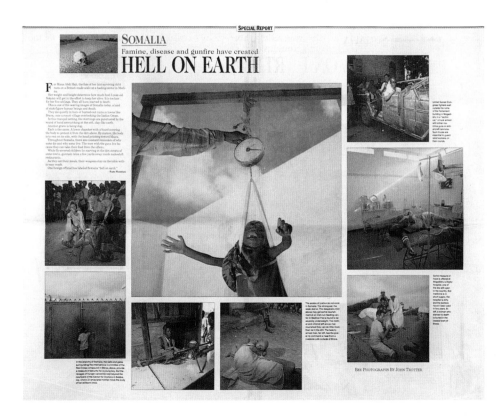

Award of Excellence

The Sacramento Bee

Sacramento, CA

Edward Canale, AME Graphics/Features; Mark Morris, Photography Director; John Trotter,
Photographer; Lisa Roberts, Graphics Editor; Rick Shaw, Graphics Editor

Silver & JSR
The New York Times
Staff

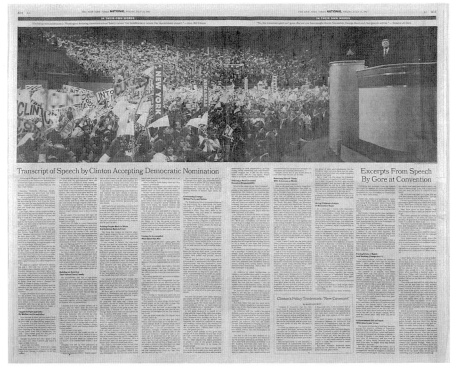

Bronze & JSR

The New York Times

Staff

Gold & JSR

The New York Times

Staff

"All the News That's Fit to Print"

The New York Times

Late Edition

New York: **Today,** brightening after morning fog. High 66. **Tonight,** rain arriving. **Tomorrow,** variable clouds, breezy, cooler. High 60. **Yesterday,** high 55, low 49. Details, page C17.

VOL.CXLII . No. 49,140 — Copyright © 1992 The New York Times — *NEW YORK, WEDNESDAY, NOVEMBER 4, 1992* — *50 CENTS*

CLINTON CAPTURES PRESIDENCY WITH HUGE ELECTORAL MARGIN; WINS A DEMOCRATIC CONGRESS

OTHER HIGHLIGHTS

Braun — Murray — Feinstein

WOMEN IN THE SENATE

'Year of the Woman,' as Predicted

This was to be the "Year of the Woman," and that prediction was borne out in the Senate elections. Carol Moseley Braun, a Chicago Democrat, will be the first black woman in the Senate.

In California, two women were elected to the Senate at once: Dianne Feinstein, the former Mayor of San Francisco, who won a special election to fill the last two years of Gov. Pete Wilson's Senate term; and Representative Barbara Boxer, who won a full six-year term to succeed Alan Cranston. Both are Democrats.

In Washington State, Patty Murray, a Democrat, defeated a five-term Republican Congressman.

But Lynn Yeakel of Pennsylvania, the Democrat who won her primary on a tide of anger over the Clarence Thomas-Anita Hill hearings, fell short in her challenge to Senator Arlen Specter.

SENATE

Newcomers, Upsets And Familiar Faces

Campbell

Ben Nighthorse Campbell, a Democrat, won in Colorado; he will be the Senate's first American Indian.

In Wisconsin, another Democrat, State Senator Russell Feingold, beat Senator Bob Kasten.

Only one Democratic incumbent, Senator Terry Sanford of North Carolina, was defeated; he lost to a one-time close friend, Lauch Faircloth. Two other Southern Democrats who faced tough races, Ernest F. Hollings Jr. of South Carolina and Wyche Fowler of Georgia, survived. So did John Glenn in Ohio, who defeated Lieut. Gov. Michael DeWine in the toughest race of his career.

HOUSE

On Capitol Hill, A Big Freshman Class

In state after state, Democratic lawmakers who clung to Bill Clinton's coattails survived tough Republican challenges. But there will be more than 100 new members in the 103d Congress. They are sure to change the face of Congress, with sharp increases in the numbers of women, blacks and Hispanic lawmakers. Several black women were elected to represent Congressional districts in the South.

THE REGION

Dodd Wins 3d Term; Green and Downey Lose

Senator Christopher J. Dodd, the Connecticut Democrat, turned back a challenge from a businessman, Brook Johnson.

But Thomas J. Downey, a Long Island Democrat whose 18 years in the House made him one of its most influential members, lost to Rick Lazio, a Suffolk County Legislator who had made Mr. Downey's overdrawn checks at the House bank a major issue in his campaign.

New York City's liberal Republican Congressman, Bill Green, lost the seat he has held for seven terms to Carolyn B. Maloney, an upstart Democrat.

BALLOT ISSUES

Return Incumbents? Not Forever, Voters Say

In a display of anti-Washington passions, voters in at least five states — Florida, Michigan, Missouri, Nebraska and Ohio — approved measures to limit the terms of members of the House and Senate. But those measures face an uncertain future in the courts.

THE ELECTIONS: SECTION B

National Coverage	B1-7
State by State	B8-10
The New York Region	B12-16
Other Metropolitan News	B17-19

Bill and Hillary Clinton at a Fort Worth rally, hours before the Governor became President-elect. Associated Press

A Man Who Wants to Be Liked, and Is

William Jefferson Blythe Clinton

By MICHAEL KELLY

Man in the News

It is 2:30 in the morning of Election Day, and Bill Clinton, a middling amateur saxophonist, is playing his true instrument, the crowd.

Thousands of people have come to see him in Fort Worth, and they are wild with emotion, straining so heavily against the heavy steel barricades set up to keep them apart from the candidate that it takes half a dozen large police officers to keep the fences from toppling forward.

The candidate, his boyish face beaming in the moonlight, plunges along the line, grabbing every hand he can, reaching up over the heads to touch in the second and third ranks. The crowd swells and surges as he goes by. In the press, a young woman faints, slumping blank-eyed to the tarmac, but Mr. Clinton is already 10 feet away, still moving and touching, and he doesn't notice.

Garry Mauro, Mr. Clinton's Texas campaign manager and a friend since he and Mr. Clinton entered politics working in the 1972 Presidential campaign of George McGovern in this state, watches in mild wonder. "He's decided he doesn't want to be President," Mr. Mauro says. "He wants to be a rock star."

The communion between William Jefferson Blythe Clinton and the people is the central fact of his life, and of his race for the goal he pursued for three decades, the Presidency.

Thirteen months ago, when Mr. Clinton stood in front of the Old State Capitol in Little Rock and announced his candidacy, he was considered by many an unlikely prospect. He had been elected to five terms as Governor of Arkansas, but running a state with an annual budget smaller than that of the District of Columbia did not seem much of a qualification. Republicans dismissed him, and the Democrats, hoping to regain the White House that had been denied to them for 12 years, pined for someone more glamorous.

After an old friend named Gennifer Flowers and an old letter by the young Bill Clinton raised questions about his integrity, the consensus grew that the candidate was dead, and would be buried in time.

Mr. Clinton, who was always the chief strategist of his campaign, banked on the central faith of his political life: If he could meet enough people, talk to enough people, make the essential connection enough times, he would win. The people

Continued on Page B2, Column 1

BUSH PLEDGES HELP

Governor Given an Edge of 43% to 38%, With Perot Getting 18%

By ROBIN TONER

Gov. Bill Clinton of Arkansas was elected the 42d President of the United States yesterday, breaking a 12-year Republican hold on the White House.

Mr. Clinton shattered the Republicans' political base with a promise of change to an electorate clearly discontented with President Bush.

Ross Perot, the Texas billionaire who roiled this race throughout, finished third, drawing roughly equally from both major party candidates, according to Voter Research & Surveys, the television polling consortium. His share of the popular vote had the potential to exceed any third-party candidate's in more than half a century.

Faithful Are Won Back

The President-elect, capping an astonishing political comeback for the Democrats over the last 18 months, ran strongly in all regions of the country and among many groups that were key to the Republicans' dominance of the 1980's: Catholics, suburbanites, independents, moderates and the Democrats who crossed party lines in the 1980's to vote for Ronald Reagan and Mr. Bush.

The Governor from Arkansas won such big, closely contested states as Michigan, Missouri, Pennsylvania, New Jersey and Illinois. As polls closed across the nation, networks announced projected winners based on voter surveys. It was Ohio that put him over the top shortly before 11 P.M., followed closely by California. Based on those projections, Mr. Bush prevailed in his adopted state of Texas and other pockets of Republican states around the country.

With 83 percent of the nation's precincts reporting by 3 A.M. today, Mr. Clinton had 43 percent to 38 percent for Mr. Bush and 18 percent for Mr. Perot.

A state-by-state breakdown of those returns gave the President-elect more than 345 electoral votes, a commanding victory in the Electoral College, which requires 270 for election. His victory also provided coattails for Democrats running for Congress in the face of tough Republican challenges: Democrats, who control both chambers, appeared likely to gain in the Senate and suffer manageable losses in the House.

'With High Hopes'

In a victory speech to a joyous crowd in Little Rock, Mr. Clinton declared, "On this day, with high hopes and brave hearts, in massive numbers, the American people have voted to make a new beginning."

He described the election as a "clari-

Continued on Page B6, Column 1

D'Amato Is Victor Over Abrams In New York's Bitter Senate Race

By TODD S. PURDUM

Senator Alfonse M. D'Amato, the battle-scarred Republican incumbent, drew support from just enough Democrats to squeak to a third term over State Attorney General Robert Abrams last night, claiming victory despite an overwhelming landslide for Bill Clinton in New York.

Mr. D'Amato won re-election, after repeated investigations into his conduct in office, in the tightest statewide contest since his own initial victory in a three-way race 12 years ago, according to unofficial returns.

With 97 percent of election districts reporting at 1:30 A.M. today, the vote was:

D'Amato	2,944,182 (51%)
Abrams	2,849,671 (49%)

At 1:20 A.M., Mr. D'Amato appeared in a ballroom of the New York Hilton and Towers, flanked by his mother, Antoinette, and former Mayor Edward I. Koch, and proclaimed proudly: "I'm not a diplomat. I'm your advocate, and I'm going to continue the fight."

The closeness of the race was a painful blow to Mr. Abrams in the face of Mr. Clinton's strength in a state where registered Democrats outnumber Republicans by nearly 3 to 2, and a testament to the fury of a contest in which Mr. D'Amato not only outspent Mr. Abrams by 2 to 1 but also outmaneuvered him at almost every turn in the costliest Senate race in the nation this year. At 2 A.M., Mr. Abrams told supporters in a ballroom of the Sheraton New York that Mr. D'Amato appeared to have won and congratulated him. But he left open the possibility that a final count, including paper and

Continued on Page B12, Column 1

INSIDE

Abortion Curb Is Voided

A Federal appeals court invalidated the Administration's ban on abortion counseling at Government-financed family planning clinics. Page A29.

Report on Women in Combat

A Presidential panel said women should be allowed to serve on most warships but be barred from combat flights and ground fighting. Page A24.

News Summary	A2
Obituaries	D24-25
Weather	C17

Arts	C17-24	Media	D20
Bridge	C17	Op-Ed	A31
Chronicle	B19	Politics	B1-16
Crossword	C21	Real Estate	D22
Editorials	A30	Sports	B20-24
Education	D23	TV Listings	C23
Health	C16	Word and Image	C21
Classified	DN	Auto Exchange	D25

President Bush conceding defeat last night in Houston. Associated Press

Congress at a Glance

As of 2:45 A.M. Eastern time

	Current balance	At stake	Winners	New balance
SENATE	57 Dem. 43 Rep.	19 Dem. 15 Rep.	19 Dem. 11 Rep. 4 Undecided	57 D, 39 R, 4 Undecided
HOUSE	268 Dem. 166 Rep. 1 Ind.	All 435 seats	222 Dem. 151 Rep. 1 Ind.	222 D, 151 R, 1 Ind., 61 Undecided

The Economy's Casualty

By R. W. APPLE Jr.

News Analysis

In the end it was the faltering economy, which had bedeviled him all year, that did George Bush in.

From the New Hampshire primary in February, through the party conventions this summer, to the start of the general-election campaign on Labor Day, public opinion held remarkably steady: three-quarters of the American people, according to New York Times/CBS News polls, disapproved of the way the President was handling the economy.

Mr. Bush failed to change their minds with his furious closing onslaught against Bill Clinton's character. More than 7 voters in 10 said in interviews as they left their polling places yesterday that they considered the economy not so good or poor, and a big majority opted for giving the Arkansas Governor a chance to turn it around. Though many had doubts about a man untried on the national stage, they had lost faith in Mr. Bush's ability to do the job, and they found Ross Perot too much of a gamble.

Electoral votes piled up in landslide proportions as Mr. Clinton blitzed through some of the most hotly contested terrain in this election: New Jersey, Pennsylvania, Michigan, Ohio, Illinois and Missouri. He swept New England and the West Coast states of California, Oregon and Washington. With that kind of triumph, leading Democrats said, the pressure on Mr. Clinton to produce big economic improvements soon after taking office will be enormous.

Competing Imperatives

Within days of moving into the White House, for example, he will have to find a balance between competing imperatives: getting a start on reducing the deficit and finding some way to jump-start the nation's stalled economic engine. With Democrats firmly in control of the House and Senate once again, the President-elect will have little excuse for inaction or confusion.

If the partisan coloration of the new Congress will be little different, its diversity will be markedly greater, with four more women and an American Indian, the first ever, in the Senate,

Continued on Page B3, Column 1

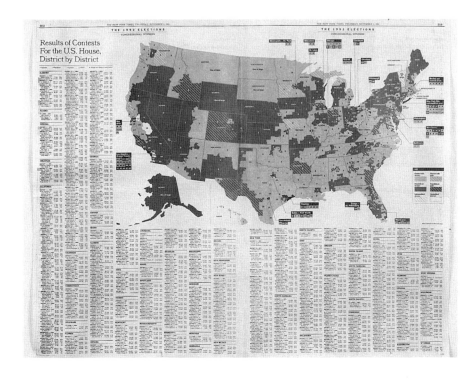

Silver

El Norte

Monterrey, Mexico

Ileana Gorostieta, Designer;
Raul Braulio Martinez,
Designer; Gustavo Ramirez,
Designer; Arturo Rangel,
Illustrator

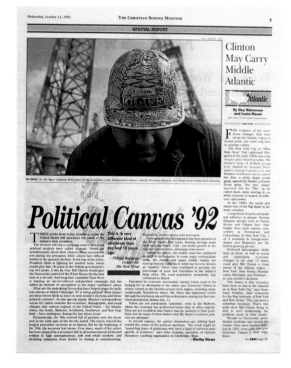

Award of Excellence
San Francisco Examiner

Kelly Frankeny, Art Director; Bob McLeod, Photo
Director; Staff

Award of Excellence
The Christian Science Monitor

John Van Pelt, Design Director; Shirley Horn, Graphics Artist; Joan
Rapaport, Graphics Artist; Neal J. Menschel, Photo Director

Award of Excellence
The Orange County Register
Santa Ana, CA

John Fabris, Assistant News Editor/Design; Karen Kelso,
Assistant News Editor/Design; David Medzerian, Assistant News
Editor/Design; Brenda Shoun, Assistant News Editor/Design;
Claudia Guerrero, Designer; Kevin Byrne, News Editor/Design;
Venetia Lai, News Editor/Visuals (Graphics); Ron Londen, News
Editor/Visuals (Photo); Nanette Bisher, AME/Art Director; Staff

Award of Excellence
The Wichita Eagle
Wichita, KS

Staff

Award of Excellence
The Seattle Times

Greg Rasa, Designer; David Miller, Art Director & Designer; Fred Birchman, Designer; James McFarlane, Designer; Phyllis Winfield, Designer; Dave Felthouse, Designer; David de la Fuente, Designer

Award of Excellence
Calgary Herald

Calgary, Alberta, Canada

Dick Wallace, Art Director; Roger Watanabe, Art Director & Illustrator; Rob Dudley, Designer

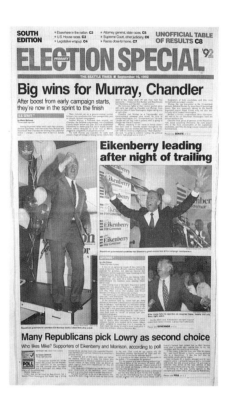

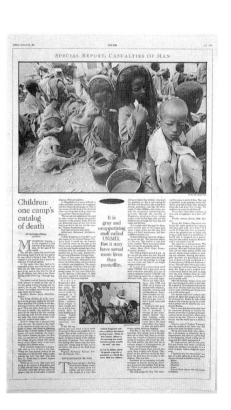

Award of Excellence
The Times-Picayune

New Orleans, LA

Kurt Mutchler, Graphics Editor; George Berke, Design Director; Billy Turner, Assistant Sports Editor; Doug Parker, Assistant Photo Editor; Dinah Rogers, Assistant Photo Editor; Tom Gregory, Associate Editor News

Award of Excellence
The Baltimore Sun

Cotton Coulson, Photo Editor; John Goecke, AME Graphics/Photography; Joe Hutchinson, Graphics Director

Silver

The Orange County Register

Santa Ana, CA

John Fabris, Assistant News Editor/Design; David Medzerian, Assistant News Editor/Design; Brenda Shoun, Assistant News Editor/Design; Michele Cardon, Picture Editor; Kevin Byrne, News Editor/Design; Venetia Lai, News Editor/Visuals (Graphics); Ron Londen, News Editor/Visuals (Photo); Nanette Bisher, AME/Art Director; Tonnie Katz, Managing Editor; Staff

Bronze

Maine Sunday Telegram

Portland, ME

Rick Wakely, Graphics Editor & Designer; Andrea Philbrick, Design Editor; Sandy Shriver, Photo Editor; John Patriquin, Photographer; Pete Gorski, Illustrator

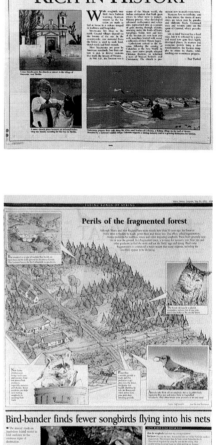

Prison care turns veteran into casualty

Willie Matheny's pain and suffering costs taxpayers nearly a half-million dollars

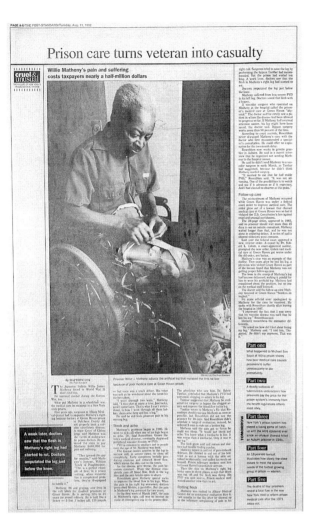

Bronze

The Post-Standard

Syracuse, NY

Michael A. Braia, Staff Artist; Susan Santola, Art Director; Tim Reese, Photographer

Ex-cop dies of neglect in prison

Larry Inslee' life began to unravel with the onset of manic depression

One prison improves after 15-year court struggle

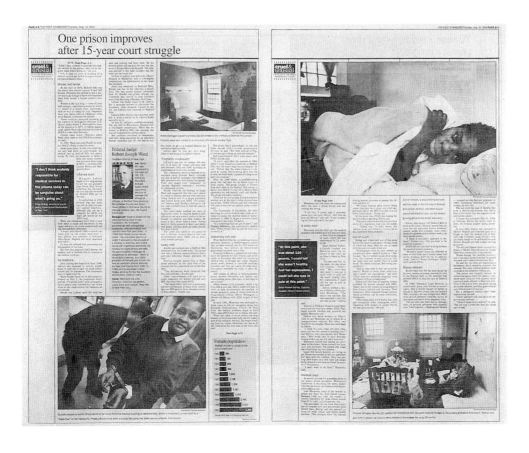

Award of Excellence

The Detroit News

Dale Peskin, AME; Dierck Casselman, AME; Nancy Hanus,
Assistant News Editor; Joe Gray, Assistant News Editor; Beth
Valone, Assistant News Editor

Award of Excellence

The Detroit News

Dale Peskin, AME; Mark Lett, AME; Joe Gray,
Assistant News Editor; Nancy Hanus, Assistant News
Editor; Mary Harris, Assistant Business Editor

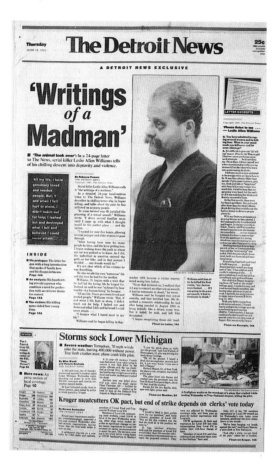

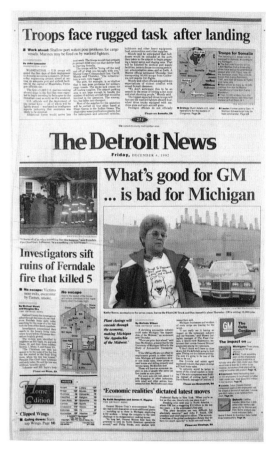

Award of Excellence

Star Tribune

Minneapolis, MN

Billy Steve Clayton, News Artist

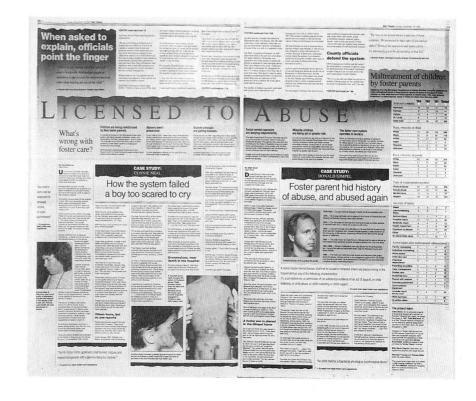

Award of Excellence
The Wichita Eagle
Wichita, KS

Sara Quinn, Designer; Dave Williams, Photographer; Richard Hernandez, Photographer; Alice Sky, News Editor/Visuals

Award of Excellence
The Wichita Eagle
Wichita, KS

Alice Sky, News Editor/Visuals; Tim Potter, Designer; Jeff Rush, Designer; Dave Williams, Photographer; Randy Tobias, Photographer; Fernando Salazar, Photographer; Richard Hernandez, Photographer; Sara Quinn, Graphics Artist

Award of Excellence
San Francisco Chronicle

Steve Kearsley, Designer; Bruce Krefting, Graphics Artist; Kristine Strawser, Graphics Artist; John Boring, Graphics Artist; Bill Smith, Graphics Artist; Lourdes Livingston, Illustrator; Alyx Meltzer, Graphics Researcher; Steve Outing, Graphics Editor

Silver & JSR

The New York Times
Ken McFarlin, Art Director & Designer

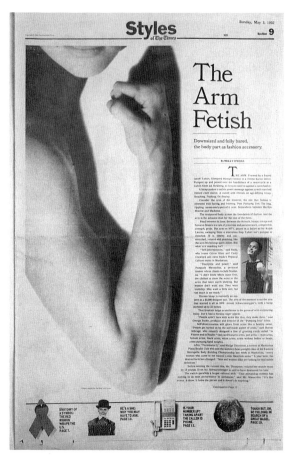

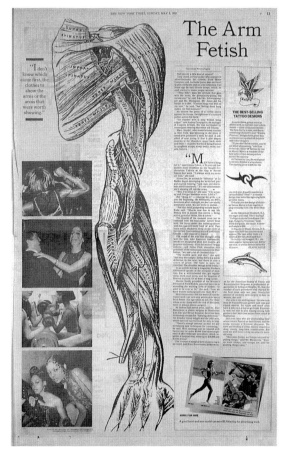

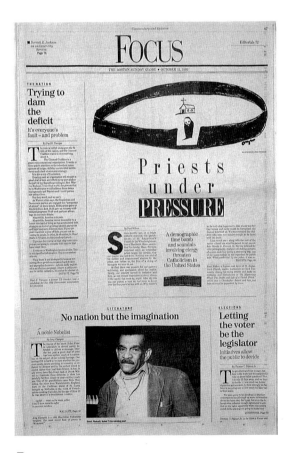

Award of Excellence

Seattle Post-Intelligencer

Ben Garrison, Duane Hoffmann Dave Gray, Steve Greenberg

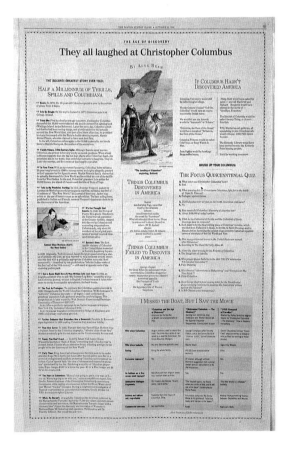

Bronze

The Boston Globe

Cynthia Hoffman, Art Director & Designer; Mark Feeney, Editor; Lynn Staley, Art Director & Designer

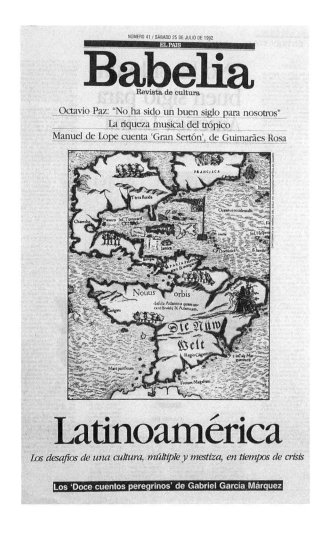

Bronze

El Pais

Madrid, Spain

Luis Galan, Designer; Teresa Fuente, Designer; J. Ignacio
Tamargo, Designer

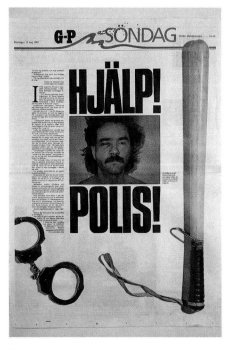

Bronze

Philadelphia Daily News

John Sherlock, Graphics Editor; Dominic Wolocko, Designer; Sandra Shea,
Section Editor

Award of Excellence

The Washington Times

Joseph Scopin, Art Director; Dolores Motichka, Art
Director & Designer (Books); Paul Watts, Designer;
Alexander Hunter, Art Director & Designer
(Commentary)

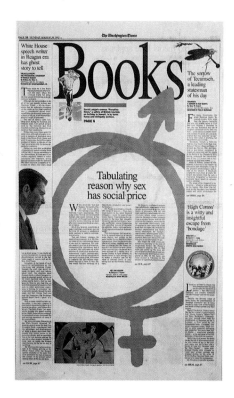

Silver

Diario 16

Madrid, Spain

Carlos Perez Diaz, Art Director & Designer; Montserrat Ortiz, Designer

MALEK IN ACTION?

O n one strategic New Hampshire day before the state's primary, Patrick Buchanan announced his candidacy, President Bush opened his campaign office in the state, and the Small Business Administration (SBA) announced a multi-billion dollar plan to aid beleaguered New Hampshire businesses.

Democrats and even SBA staff accused the president of using federal funds to aid in his re-election. Although no evidence ties this maneuver to Fred Malek, Bush's campaign manager, the move bears a striking resemblance to Malek's Watergate-era Responsiveness Program — a plan that in part directed federal grants where they would win votes for Nixon.

"The SBA has had to re-target quickly diminishing resources to one small state whose chief virtue seems to be an early primary," wrote Democratic congressman Ron Wyden, chairman of the subcommittee on regulation, business opportunities and energy, which investigated the New Hampshire loan program. Indeed, Bush was lagging behind Buchanan in the polls, and SBA administrator Patricia Saiki is a Bush appointee who might reasonably be expected to be sensitive to the president's needs. "The SBA director is a political appointee who is more than happy to comply with the administration. They are on the same team," contends Steve Jenning, staff director for Congressman Wyden's subcommittee.

New Hampshire Governor Judd Gregg put his foot in his mouth when he told reporters that his state was graced with the program because he "was in the right party" — making it sound exactly like a political payoff. Under the New Hampshire Pilot Lending Program, which was scheduled to encompass the rest of New England within months, the federal government would guarantee private-sector high-risk loans made to small businesses. If the businesses went under, the SBA would pay back the loan — a no-risk incentive for private lenders.

But the SBA initiated the program knowing it couldn't afford to cover the extra loans, and that the program would decrease the guaranteed support in loans made throughout the rest of the country. Outside of New Hampshire, small businesses would suffer. Says Congressman Wyden, "When small businesses are hurting across the country in Texas or Portland, programs ought to be based on merit. This is a program based on politics."

Sure enough, the program ran out of money before it had even reached the rest of New England. "This was a grotesque example of naked politics — the use of government resources for political purposes. The money went in right before the primary and ran out right after," says John Weiner, counsel to Democratic Senator John Kerry of Massachusetts, who publicly lambasted the SBA plan. "This is exactly the kind of thing that the Nixon administration was disliked for."

When questioned about the New Hampshire Pilot Lending Program, Malek claimed to know little about it. Then he said he had to get off the phone.

AUGUST 13, 1992 • HOUSTON PRESS 39

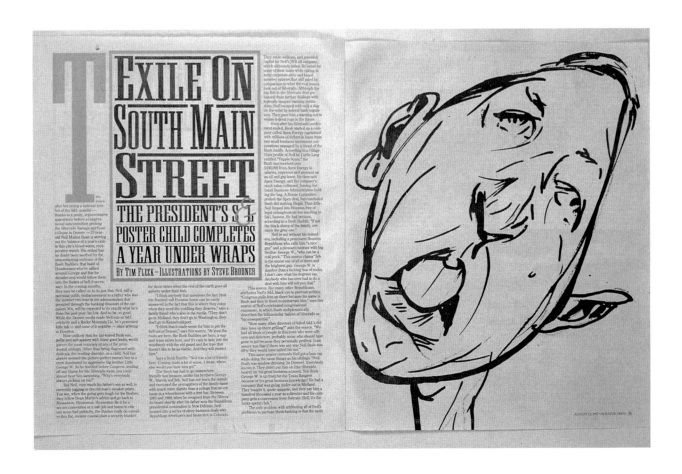

EXILE ON SOUTH MAIN STREET

THE PRESIDENT'S S&L POSTER CHILD COMPLETES A YEAR UNDER WRAPS

BY TIM FLECK — ILLUSTRATIONS BY STEVE BRODNER

AUGUST 13, 1992 • HOUSTON PRESS 35

Silver
Houston Press

Audrey Satterwhite, Art Director; Ted Keller, Associate Art Director; Chris Hearne, Publisher; John Wilburn, Editor; Steve Brodner, Illustrator

Silver

The Toronto Star

Evelyn Stoynoff, Designer; Patti Gower, Photographer; Andrew Stawicki, Photographer; Jimmy Atkins, Editor

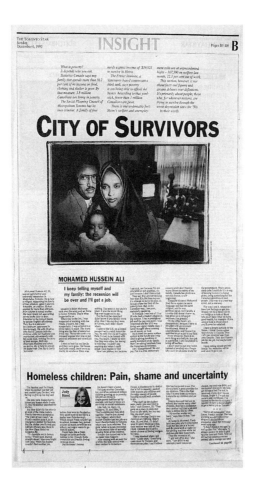

Bronze & JSR

El Mundo

Madrid, Spain

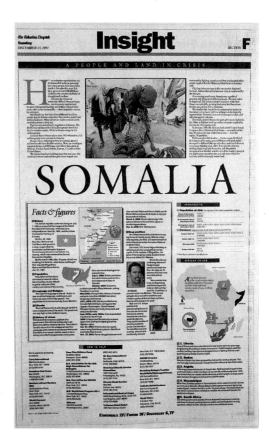

Bronze

The Columbus Dispatch

Columbus, OH

Scott Minister, Art Director & Designer; Doug Miller, Infographics Artist; Nancy McCloud, Infographics Artist; Owen DeWolfe, Section Editor

Bronze

The Miami Herald

Patterson Clark, Graphics Artist; Randy Stano, Director/Editorial Art & Design; Rich Bard, Viewpoint Editor

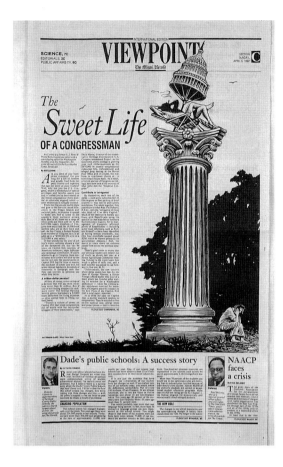

Award of Excellence

New Times

Phoenix, AZ

Brian Stauffer, Art Director; Timothy Archibald, Photographer

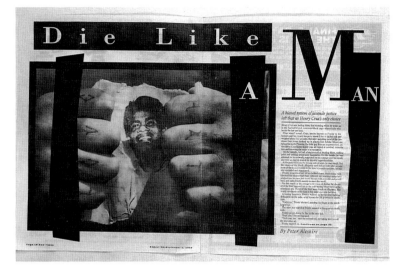

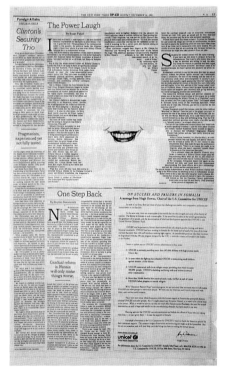

Award of Excellence

The Globe and Mail

Toronto, Canada

Eric Nelson, Art Director & Designer; Sarah Murdoch, Editor; Paula Sten, Photographer

Award of Excellence

Los Angeles Times

Sandra Chelist, Art Director & Designer; Matt Mahurin, Illustrator

Award of Excellence

The New York Times

Mirko Ilic, Art Director & Designer; Corinne Myller, Designer; Ruth Marten, Illustrator

Award of Excellence

The UCSD Guardian

La Jolla, CA

James Collier, Designer; Ben Boychuk, Editor; Mel Marcelo, Graphics Editor; Katherine Roe, Graphics Artist

Award of Excellence

The Columbus Dispatch

Columbus, OH

Kathy Dlabick, Designer; Eric Albrecht, Photographer; Owen DeWolfe, Insight Editor

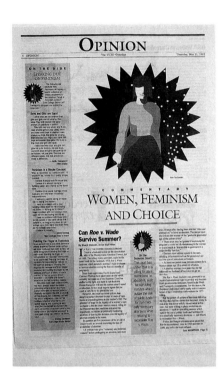

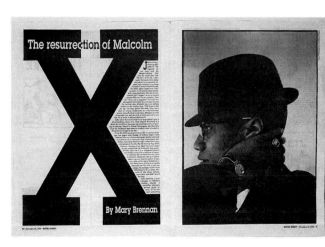

Award of Excellence

New Times

Phoenix, AZ

Brian Stauffer, Art Director; Timothy Archibald, Photographer; Kim Klein, Design Director

Award of Excellence

Seattle Weekly

Seattle, WA

Fred Andrews, Art Director

Gold

El Nuevo Herald

Miami, FL

Armando Alvarez, Bravo Author; Raul Fernandez, Illustrator/Designer; Nuri Ducassi, Art Director

THE BEST OF NEWSPAPER DESIGN **99**

Silver

El Norte

Monterrey, Mexico

Arturo Jimenez, Designer

Silver

El Nuevo Herald

Miami, FL

Nuri Ducassi, Art Director/Designer/Illustrator

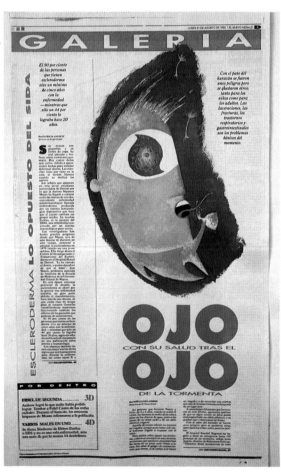

Silver

El Nuevo Herald

Miami, FL

Nuri Ducassi, Art Director/Designer/Illustrator

Award of Excellence
Detroit Free Press
Keith Webb, Designer

Award of Excellence
El Nuevo Herald
Miami, FL
Jose Pacheco Silva, Designer; Nuri Ducassi, Art Director; Silvia Licha, Editor

Award of Excellence
El Nuevo Herald
Miami, FL
Jose Pacheco Silva, Designer; Nuri Ducassi, Art Director; Silvia Licha, Editor

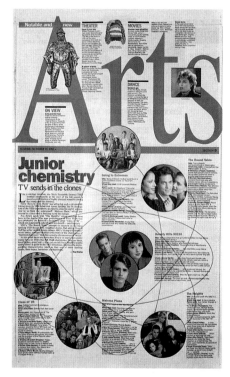

Award of Excellence
El Nuevo Herald
Miami, FL
Nuri Ducassi, Art Director & Designer

Award of Excellence
El Nuevo Herald
Miami, FL
Nuri Ducassi, Art Director & Designer

Award of Excellence
The Washington Times
John Kascht, Art Director & Designer

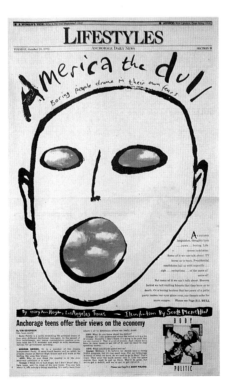

Silver

Anchorage Daily News

Galie Jean-Louis, Features Design Director; Timothy White, Photographer

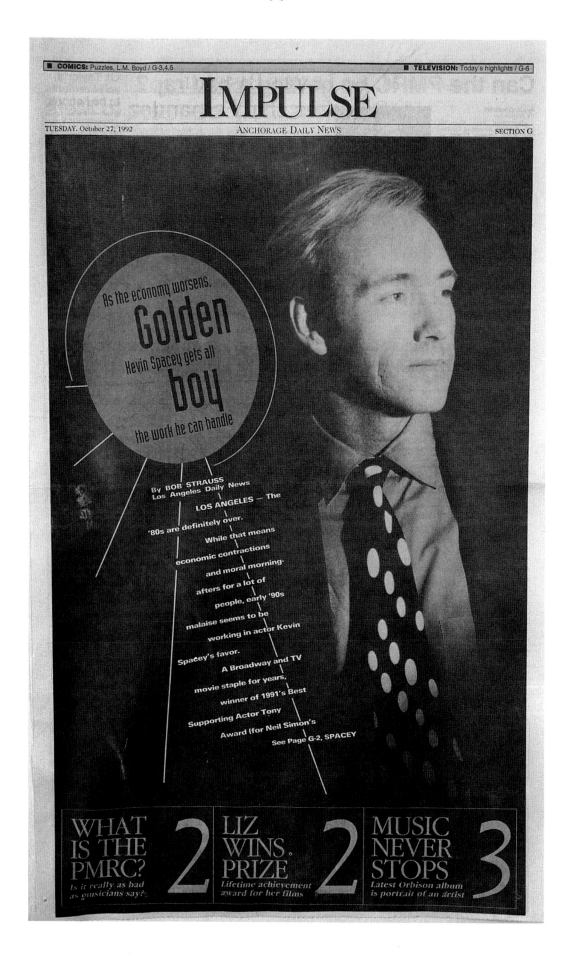

Bronze

The Charlotte Observer

Charlotte, NC

Sarah Blaydon, Designer; Al Phillips, Illustrator; Laura Mueller, Photographer

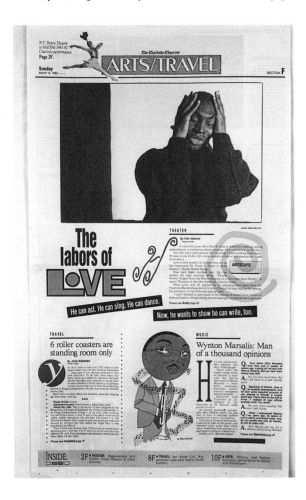

Bronze

Anchorage Daily News

Galie Jean-Louis, Features Design Director/Designer

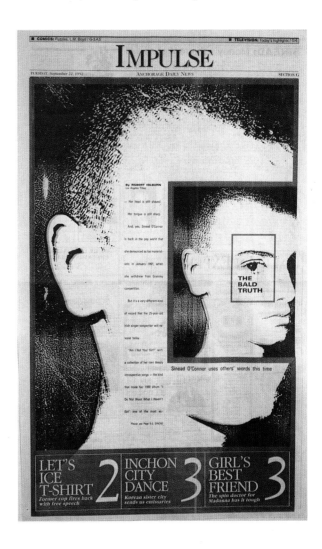

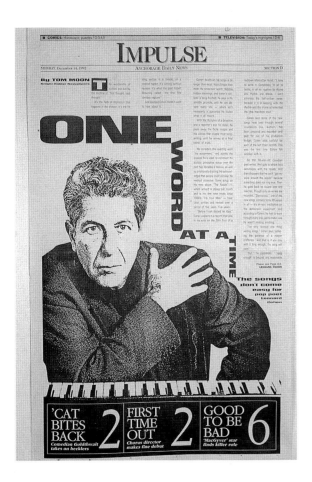

Bronze

Anchorage Daily News

Galie Jean-Louis, Features Design Director; Dee Boyles, Features

Award of Excellence

The Akron Beacon Journal

Akron, OH

Ted Schneider, Designer; Dennis Balogh, Illustrator & Designer

Award of Excellence

Anchorage Daily News

Galie Jean-Louis, Features Design Director & Designer; Joel Nakamura, Illustrator

Award of Excellence

Anchorage Daily News

Galie Jean-Louis, Features Design Director & Designer; Scott Menchin, Illustrator

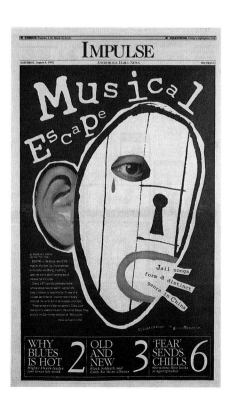

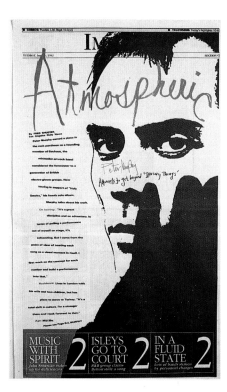

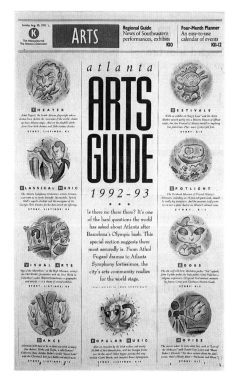

Award of Excellence

Anchorage Daily News

Galie Jean-Louis, Features Design Director; Dee Boyles, Designer

Award of Excellence

Anchorage Daily News

Galie Jean-Louis, Designer & Features Design Director

Award of Excellence

The Atlanta Journal/Constitution

Peter Dishal, Designer; John Amoss, Illustrator; Mike Gordon, Design Director; Tony De Feria, Art Director

Award of Excellence
The Boston Globe

Rena Sokolow, Art Director & Designer; Rico Lins,
Illustrator

Award of Excellence
The Boston Globe

Cynthia Hoffman, Art Director & Designer; Staff
Photographers

Award of Excellence
The Charlotte Observer

Charlotte, NC

Sarah Blaydon, Designer; Mark Sluder, Photographer

Award of Excellence
Dayton Daily News

Dayton, OH

Don Reynolds, Designer

Award of Excellence
The Detroit News

Glynis Sweeny, Illustrator & Designer; Wes Bausmith,
Art Director

Award of Excellence
The Detroit News

Glynis Sweeny, Illustrator & Designer; Wes Bausmith,
Art Director

Award of Excellence
The New York Times

Genevieve Williams, Art Director & Designer; Roy
Lichtenstein, Sculpture; Jo Teodorescu, Illustrator

Award of Excellence
The New York Times

Linda Brewer, Art Director & Designer; Daniel Watson,
Photographer/ABC

Award of Excellence
The Lowell Sun

Lowell, MA

Mitchell J. Hayes, Art Director & Designer; Burton

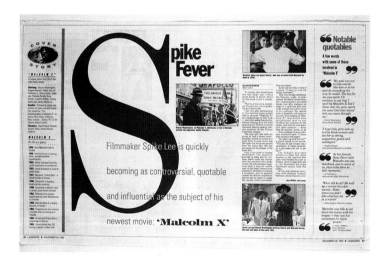

Award of Excellence
The Times-Picayune

New Orleans, LA

Beth Aguillard, Designer; Jean McIntosh, Art Director; Kurt Mutchler, Graphics Editor

Award of Excellence
The Ann Arbor News

Ann Arbor, MI
Michael McGowan, Graphics Artist

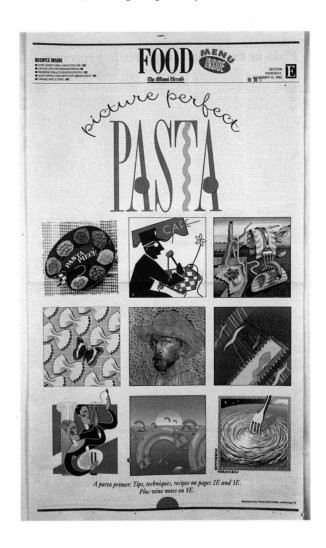

Bronze
The Boston Globe

Susan Dawson, Designer; Yunghi Kim, Photographer; Dave Brady,
Illustrator; Maxine Boll, Illustrator

Bronze
The Detroit News

Glynis Sweeny, Designer/Illustrator; Wes Bausmith, Art Director

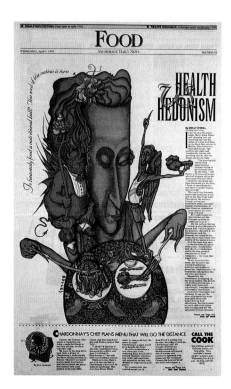

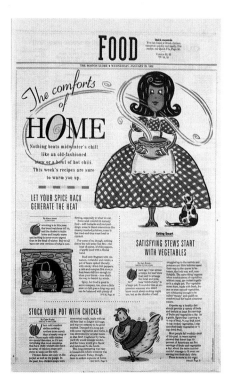

Award of Excellence
Anchorage Daily News

Galie Jean-Louis, Features Design Director; Dee Boyles,
Features Designer & Illustrator

Award of Excellence
Anchorage Daily News

Galie Jean-Louis, Features Design Director; Dee Boyles,
Illustrator & Designer; Tim Carroll, Illustrator

Award of Excellence
The Boston Globe

Lynn Staley, Designer; Holly Nixholm, Designer; Mary
Lynn Blausotta, Illustrator; Evelynne Kramer, Editor

Award of Excellence
The Miami Herald

Alex Leary, Illustrator; Felicia Gressette, Food Editor;
Rhonda Prast, Features Design; Randy Stano,
Director/Editorial Art & Design

Award of Excellence
The Miami Herald

Herman Vega, Designer; Patterson Clark, Illustrator;
Felicia Gressette, Food Editor; Randy Stano,
Director/Editorial Art & Design

Award of Excellence
The Miami Herald

Herman Vega, Designer; Liz Heisler, Illustrator; Rhonda
Prast, Features Design Editor; Randy Stano,
Director/Editorial Art & Design

Award of Excellence
The Miami Herald
Rhonda Prast, Features Design Editor; Felicia Gressette, Food Editor

Award of Excellence
San Francisco Examiner
Don McCartney, Designer; Kelly Frankeny, Art Director; Bob McLeod, Photo Director; Lynn Forbes, Epicure Editor

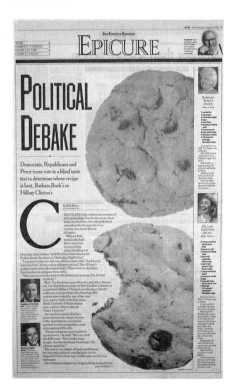

Award of Excellence
San Francisco Examiner
Don McCartney, Designer; Kelly Frankeny, Art Director

Award of Excellence
The Star-Ledger
Newark, NJ
Bernadette Dashiell, Art Director; Nannette Finkel Rebach, Page Designer; Linda Fowler, Section Editor; Steven Mark, Needham/Envision Photographer

Award of Excellence
The Sun
Bremerton, WA
Scott Whitcomb, Designer

Silver

El Nuevo Herald

Miami, FL

Aurura Arrue, Illustrator & Designer; Nuri Ducassi, Art Director; Silvia Licha, Editor

Bronze

El Nuevo Herald

Miami, FL

Nuri Ducassi, Art Director & Designer; Juan C. Perez, Editor

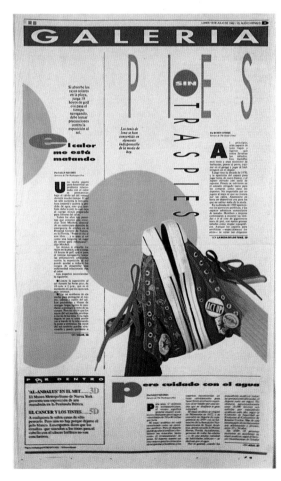

Award of Excellence
The Columbus Dispatch
Columbus, OH

Scott Minister, Art Director & Designer; Jeff Hinckley, Photographer; Becky Kover, Section Coordinator

Award of Excellence
Goteborg-Posten
Goteborg, Sweden

Karin Teghammar Arell, Designer; Ulf Sveningson, Illustrator

Award of Excellence
The Times-Picayune
New Orleans, LA

Beth Aguillard, Designer; Chris Bynum, Fashion Editor; Jean McIntosh, Art Director; Kathy Anderson, Photographer

Award of Excellence
Anchorage Daily News

Pamela Dunlap-Shohl, Features Designer; Lin Mitchell, Photographer; Joy Rodgers, Copy Editor; Jim Jager, Photo Editor

Bronze
Anchorage Daily News

Galie Jean-Louis, Features Design Director; Pamela Dunlap-Shohl, Features Designer; Silver Moon Graphics, Illustrator; Joy Rodgers, Copy Editor

Award of Excellence

Anchorage Daily News

Galie Jean-Louis, Features Design Director; Pamela
Dunlap-Shohl, Features Designer; Lin Mitchell,
Photographer; Joy Rodgers, Copy Editor; Galie Jean-
Louis, Photo Editor

Award of Excellence

Anchorage Daily News

Galie Jean-Louis, Features Design Director; Pamela
Dunlap-Shohl, Features Designer; Lin Mitchell,
Photographer; Joy Rodgers, Copy Editor; Galie Jean-
Louis, Photo Editor

Award of Excellence

Anchorage Daily News

Galie Jean-Louis, Features Design Director; Pamela
Dunlap-Shohl, Features Designer; Lin Mitchell,
Photographer; Joy Rodgers, Copy Editor; Galie Jean-
Louis, Photo Editor

Award of Excellence

Anchorage Daily News

Pamela Dunlap-Shol, Features Designer; Galie Jean-
Louis, Features Design Director; Lin Mitchell,
Photographer; Joy Rodgers, Copy Editor; Galie Jean-
Louis, Photo Editor

Award of Excellence

The Boston Globe

Aldona Charlton, Designer; Evelynne Kramer, Editor;
Janice Byrd, Writer; David Ryan, Photographer; Maria
Morga, Illustrator

Award of Excellence

The Boston Globe

Aldona Charlton, Designer; Evelynne Kramer, Editor;
Gary Baseman, Illustrator

Silver

El Nuevo Herald

Miami, FL

Rosa Bautista, Editor; Raul Fernandez,
Designer/Illustrator; Nuri Ducassi, Art Director

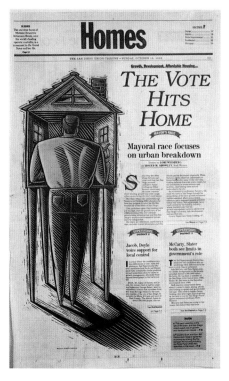

Award of Excellence

The Dallas Morning News

Marilyn A. Glaser, Designer; Natalie Caudill,
Photographer

Award of Excellence

The Miami Herald

Patterson Clark, Editorial Assistant; Jill Cassidy, Copy
Editor; Max Roberts, Section Editor; Randy Stano,
Director/Editorial Art & Design

Award of Excellence

The San Diego Union-Tribune

Laurie A Harker, Designer; Jennifer Hewitson,
Illustrator

Bronze
Akron Beacon Journal
Akron, OH

Terence Oliver, Designer/Illustrator; Ted Schneider, Designer

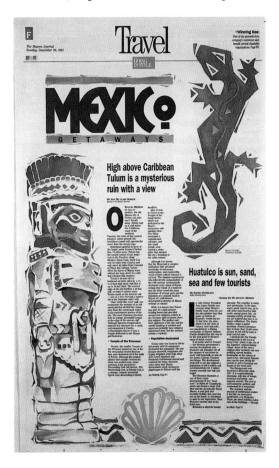

Bronze
The Boston Globe
Jacqueline Berthet, Art Director & Designer

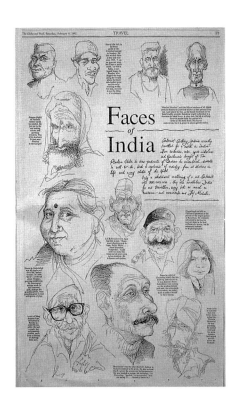

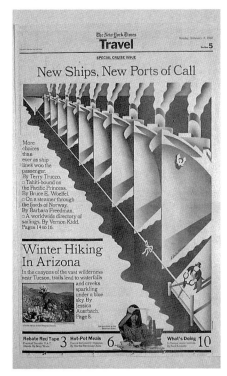

Award of Excellence
The Globe and Mail
Toronto, Canada

Gudrun Haraldsson, Art Director & Designer; Laszlo Buhasz, Editor; Anthony Jenkins, Illustrator

Award of Excellence
The Miami Herald

Ana Lense-Larrauri, Illustrator & Designer; Herman Vega, Designer; Jay Clarke, Travel Editor; Randy Stano, Director/Editorial Art & Design

Award of Excellence
The New York Times

Nick Kalish, Art Director & Designer; R. Kenton Nelson, Illustrator

Award of Excellence

The Oregonian

Portland, OR

Nancy Fullwiler Casey, Designer; Sam Hundley, Illustrator; Shawn Vitt, Art Director

Award of Excellence

San Francisco Examiner

Don McCartney, Designer; Fran Ortiz, Photographer; Kelly Frankeny, Art Director; Bob McLeod, Photo Director

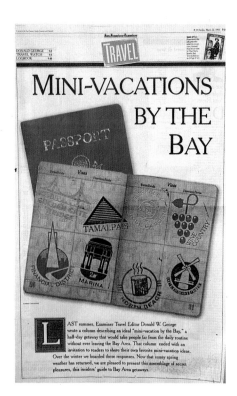

Award of Excellence

San Francisco Examiner

Don McCartney, Designer; Kelly Frankeny, Art Director; Chris Morris, Artist

Award of Excellence

The Boston Globe

Cynthia Daniels, Art Director; James Karaian, Graphics Artist

Award of Excellence

El Nuevo Herald

Miami, FL

Nuri Ducassi, Art Director, Designer & Illustrator

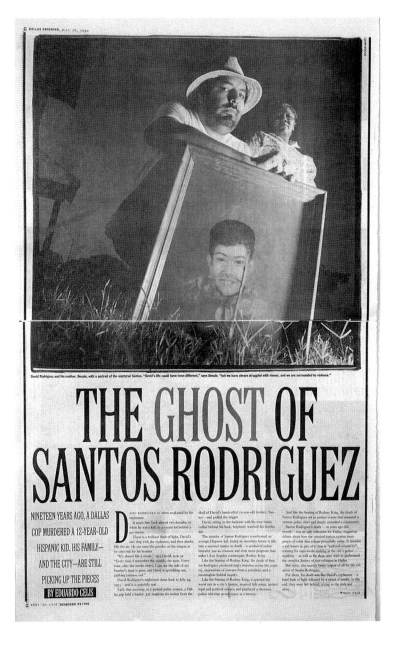

David Rodriguez and his mother, Bessie, with a portrait of the murdered Santos. "David's life could have been different," says Bessie, "but we have always struggled with money, and we are surrounded by violence."

THE GHOST OF
SANTOS RODRIGUEZ

NINETEEN YEARS AGO, A DALLAS COP MURDERED A 12-YEAR-OLD HISPANIC KID. HIS FAMILY—AND THE CITY—ARE STILL PICKING UP THE PIECES

BY EDUARDO CELIS

Bronze

Reporter

Buffalo, NY

Rebecca Farnham, Art Director

Parking Strategy

(Carol) Murphy's Law:
You Can Learn to Park Smart

Award of Excellence

Akron Beacon Journal

Akron, OH

John Backderf, Designer

Award of Excellence

Anchorage Daily News

Pete Spino, Art Director & Designer; William Duke, Illustrator

Award of Excellence

Berlingske Tidende

Copenhagen, Denmark

Gregers Jensen, Designer

Award of Excellence

City Paper

Baltimore, MD

Mark Evans, Art Director; Craig Daniels, Photographer

Award of Excellence

Dallas Observer

Dan Zedek, Art Director; Scogin Mayo, Photographer

Award of Excellence

The Lowell Sun

Lowell, MA

Mitchell J. Hayes, Art Director & Designer;
Christopher Bing, Illustrator; Cromwell Schubarth,
Editor

Award of Excellence

San Francisco Examiner

Gordon Studer, Designer/Artist; Kelly Frankeny, Art
Director

Award of Excellence

El Norte

Monterrey, Mexico

Luis Ugalde, Designer

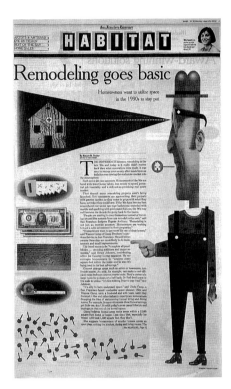

Award of Excellence

El Mundo

Madrid, Spain

Carmelo Caderot, Art Director & Designer; Manuel de
Miguel, Assistant Art Director

Award of Excellence

El Mundo

Madrid, Spain

Carmelo Caderot, Art Director & Designer; Manuel de
Miguel, Assistant Art Director

Award of Excellence

XS

Ft. Lauderdale, FL

Andrew Itkoff, Photographer; Robb Montgomery, Art
Director

Award of Excellence

Dallas Observer

Dan Zedek, Art Director; Scogin Mayo, Photographer

Award of Excellence

Houston Press

Audrey Satterwhite, Art Director; Ted Keller, Associate Art
Director; Chris Hearne, Publisher; John Wilburn, Editor; Jim
Caldwell, Photographer

Award of Excellence

American Medical News

Chicago, IL

Barbara Dow, Art Director & Designer; Stephanie
Shieldhouse, Illustrator

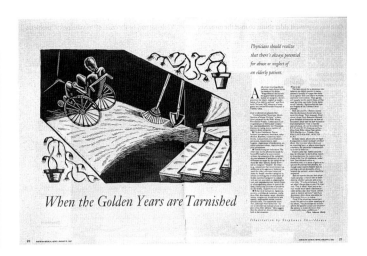

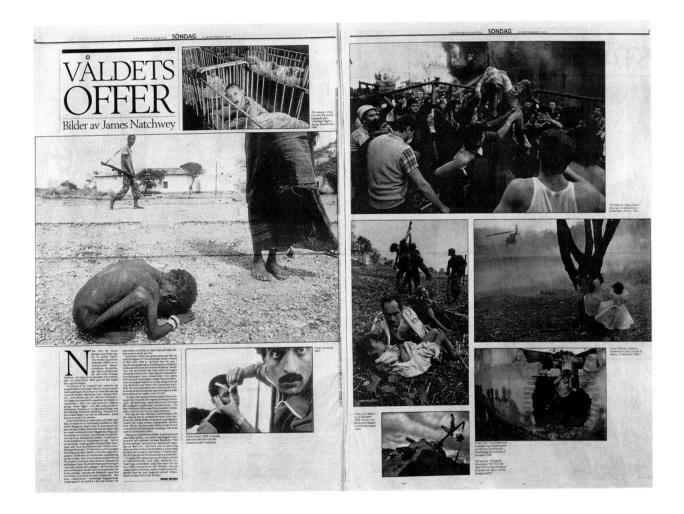

Award of Excellence

Goteborg-Posten

Goteborg, Sweden

Mats Widebrant, Designer; James Nachtwey,
Photographer

Bronze (for overall design)

El Pais Semanal

Madrid, Spain

Eugenio Gonzalez, Design Director; Isabel Benito, Designer; Gustavo Sanchez, Designer; Marta Calzada, Designer

Silver (for cover)

Angel de Pedro, Illustrator; Eugenio Gonzalez, Design Director; Isabel Benito, Designer; Gustavo Sanchez, Designer; Marta Calzada, Designer

Award of Excellence

Los Angeles Times Magazine

Nancy Duckworth, Art Director; Steven Banks, Associate Art Director; Carol Wakano, Assistant Art Director; John D'Angona, Assistant Art Director; Lisa Thackaberry, Photo Editor

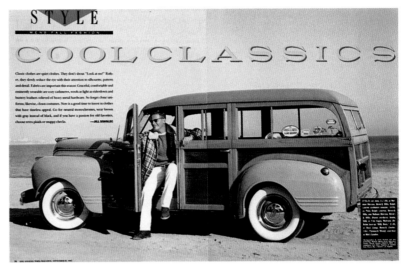

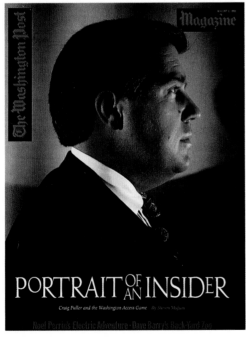

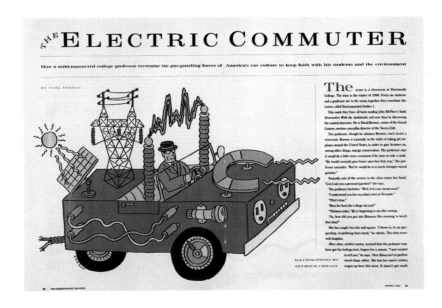

Award of Excellence

The Washington Post Magazine

Richard Baker, Art Director; Kelly Doe, Designer; Deborah Needleman, Photo Editor; Karen Tanaka, Photo Editor; Staff Illustrators & Photo Illustrator

Silver

The Akron Beacon Journal/Beacon Magazine

Akron, OH

Tim Jonke, Illustrator; Dennis Balogh, Art Director

Silver

The Boston Globe Magazine

Lucy Bartholomay, Art Director & Designer; Michele McDonald, Photographer

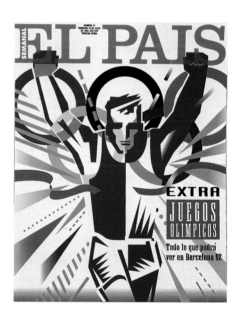

Award of Excellence

The Boston Globe Magazine

Lucy Bartholomay, Art Director & Designer; James Yang, Illustrator

Award of Excellence

The Boston Globe Magazine

Lucy Bartholomay, Art Director & Designer; Barry Blitt, Illustrator

Award of Excellence

El Pais Semanal

Madrid, Spain

Javier Romero, Illustrator; Eugenio Gonzalez, Design Director; Isabel Benito, Designer; Gustavo Sanchez, Designer; Marta Calzada, Designer

Silver

The New York Times Magazine

Janet Froelich, Art Director; Kandy Littrell, Designer; Kathy Ryan, Photo Editor; Michael O'Neill, Photographer

Silver

The Washington Post Magazine

Richard Baker, Art Director; Kelly Doe, Designer; Janet Wooley, Illustrator

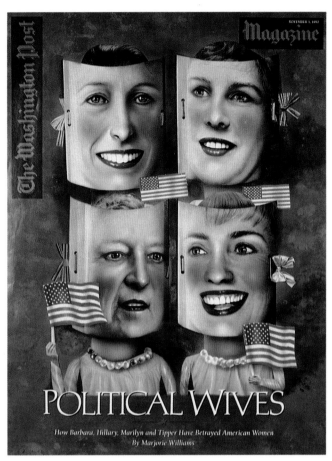

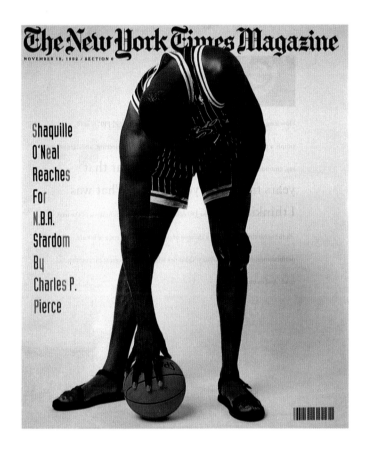

Award of Excellence

The New York Times Magazine

Tuan Dao, Art Director & Designer; Paul Lange, Photographer

Award of Excellence

St. Louis Post-Dispatch

James Cook, Artist; Tony Lazorko, News-Art Director; Amour Krupnik, AME Graphics

Silver

The Washington Post Magazine

Kelly Doe, Art Director & Designer; David Hughes,
Illustrator

Silver (for color cover)

The Washington Post Magazine

Richard Baker, Art Director & Designer; Deborah Needleman, Photo Editor; Len
Jenshel, Photographer

Bronze (for special section)

Richard Baker, Art Director & Designer; Kelly Doe, Designer; Deborah Needleman,
Photo Editor; Karen Tanaka, Photo Editor; Photographers

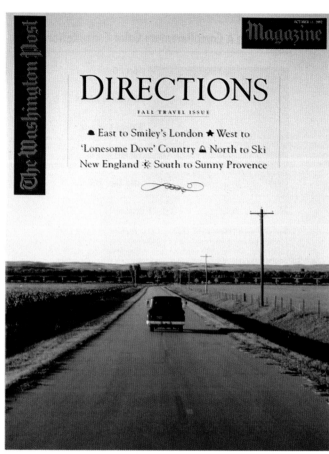

Award of Excellence

The Washington Post Magazine

Richard Baker, Art Director & Designer; David Goldin,
Illustrator

Award of Excellence

The Washington Post Magazine

Richard Baker, Art Director & Designer; Kelly Doe,
Designer; Peter De Seye, Illustrator

Award of Excellence

The Washington Post Magazine

Richard Baker, Art Director; Kelly Doe, Designer; Amy
Guip, Photo Illustrator

Bronze
Los Angeles Times Magazine

Nancy Duckworth, Art Director; Lisa Thackaberry, Photo Editor

Bronze
The Boston Globe Magazine

Lucy Bartholomay, Art Director & Designer; Scott Menchin, Illustrator

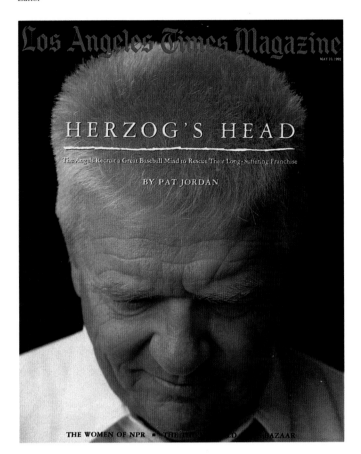

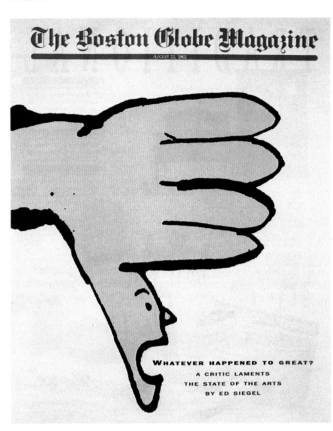

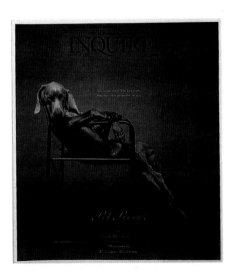

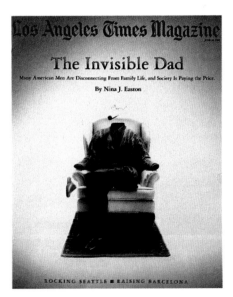

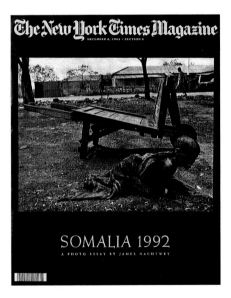

Award of Excellence
The Philadelphia Inquirer Magazine

Bert Fox, Art Director; Jessica Helfand, Design Director & Designer; William Wegman, Photographer; Bert Fox, Photo Editor

Award of Excellence
Los Angeles Times Magazine

Nancy Duckworth, Art Director; Lisa Thackaberry, Photo Editor

Award of Excellence
The New York Times Magazine

Janet Froelich, Art Director & Designer; Kathy Ryan, Photo Editor; James Nachtwey, Photographer

Silver

The Washington Post Magazine

Richard Baker, Art Director & Designer; Kelly Doe, Designer; Deborah Needleman, Photo Editor; Staff Photographers

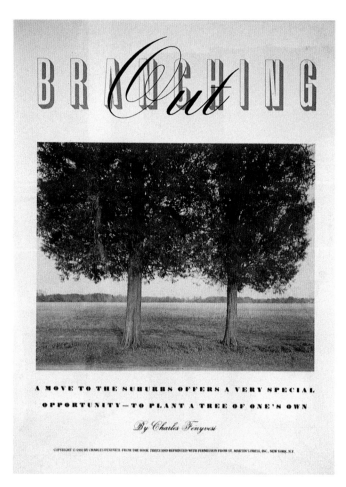

Award of Excellence

El Pais Semanal

Madrid, Spain

Soledad Alameda, Text; Jean Marie Del Moral, Photographer; Eugenio Gonzalez, Design Director; Isabel Benito, Designer; Gustavo Sanchez, Designer; Marta Calzada, Designer

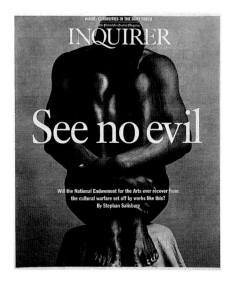

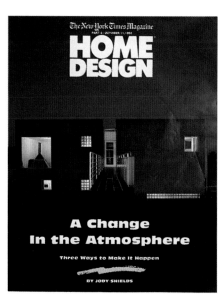

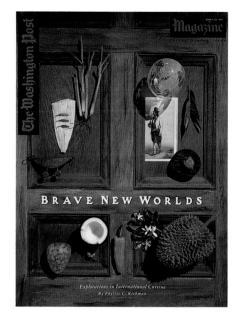

Award of Excellence

The Philadelphia Inquirer Magazine

Bert Fox, Art Director/Photo Editor; Jessica Helfand, Design Director/Designer; Robert Mapplethorpe, Photographer

Award of Excellence

The New York Times Magazine

Linda Brewer, Art Director & Designer

Award of Excellence

The Washington Post Magazine

Richard Baker, Art Director & Designer; Kelly Doe, Designer; Karen Tanaka, Photo Editor; Photographers

Silver

Los Angeles Times Magazine

Nancy Duckworth, Art Director; Steven Banks, Associate Art Director

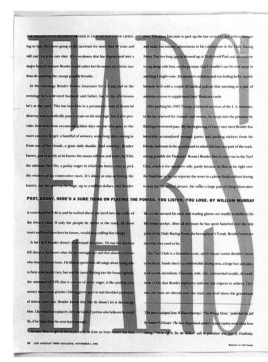

Bronze

Detroit Free Press

Claire Innes, Art Director & Designer; Patrick Corrigan, Illustrator; Deborah Withey, Design Director

Award of Excellence

Los Angeles Times Magazine

Nancy Duckworth, Art Director

Bronze
The Boston Globe Magazine

Lucy Bartholomay, Art Director & Designer; John Overmyer, Illustrator

Award of Excellence
The Boston Globe Magazine

Lucy Bartholomay, Art Director & Designer; Patrick Blackwell, Illustrator

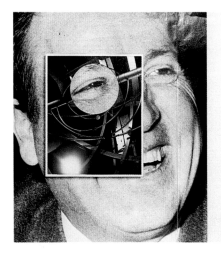

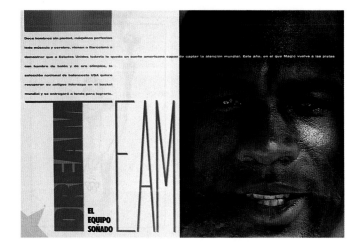

Award of Excellence
Diario 16

Madrid, Spain

Carlos Perez Diaz, Art Director & Designer; Andres Gilibert, Designer; Jose Maria Gomez, Designer

Award of Excellence
Diario 16

Madrid, Spain

Carlos Perez Diaz, Art Director & Designer; Andres Gilibert, Designer; Jose Maria Gomez

Silver

Los Angeles Times Magazine

Nancy Duckworth, Art Director; Steven Banks, Associate Art Director

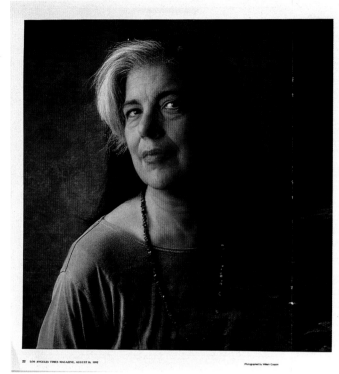

The 'Dark Lady' of American Intellectuals Ventures From Her Lofty Terrain Into

Herbert Mitgang once called her a "literary pinup." Customarily acerbic John Simon lauded her in a story titled, "The Light That Never Failed." She has been taken to task in the New Criterion for supposedly promoting a doctrine that would "release high culture from its obligations to be entirely serious." Carlos Fuentes believes her essays to be "great interpretations and even fulfillments of what is really going on." Kevin Costner's character in "Bull Durham" dismissed her novels as "self-indulgent, overrated crap." And Time magazine canonized her as someone who "has come to symbolize the writer and thinker in many variations: as analyst, rhapsodist and roving eye, as public scold and portable conscience." ● That, in a somewhat bloated nutshell, is the myth of Susan Sontag—the sphinx-like "dark lady" of American intellectuals, a myth that without aid of a single publicist's release has somehow grown and thrived for nearly 30 years. ● The *reality* of Susan Sontag is a big-boned, beautiful 59-year-old with a great guffaw

Susan Sontag Lightens Up

for a laugh and a sweetly lopsided grin. An Amazon in ratty sweats with a penchant for plopping feet on tables, giving bearhugs to any friend who walks through the door, and inviting perfect strangers to "Tell me about yourself," Sontag in the flesh is, in every way, endearing. She's a doting mother who likes to go on at length about "my son, the writer." Her speech is sprinkled with sort-ofs, kind-ofs and you-knows ("I'm a product of bad American public school education," she says, ruefully). She likes to talk to taxi drivers. ● And it is this Susan Sontag—warm, exuberant and direct, rather than her cold, obscurantic legend—that leaps off the page to greet the reader of her about-to-be-released novel, "The Volcano Lover," her first major book in three years and her first whirl at histori- cal romance. *Historical romance?* ● "When I started to write it," Sontag admits, "I thought, this is the weirdest thing I've ever written." Long limbs akimbo, Sontag is standing at ease in the blinkingly sunny Manhattan kitchen that nourishes the mind at the belly's expense (stacks of papers and books, file cabinets and fax and copying machines occupy the counters and cabinets), seemingly oblivious both to the glare and the fact that it's the most humid day of the summer. She takes a swig of hot coffee, sprawls into a chair and continues. "I thought, this book about these 18th-Century characters will have the smallest audience ever, but I'm in love and I have to do it."

the Steamy Times of an Adulteress and Her Besotted Lover • By Ellen Hopkins

LEFT: A boy in rags screams with pain as his mother squats alongside.

ABOVE: Bodies awaiting collection outside a destroyed water-pumping station, where children gather to pass the time.

RIGHT: A woman who was found lying near the pumping station is helped to a feeding center.

The most vulnerable — women, children, the elderly and the sick — are the first to perish, often killed by diseases like measles or respiratory infections that their bodies are too weak to fight off.

Silver

The New York Times Magazine

Janet Froelich, Art Director & Designer; Kathy Ryan, Photo Editor; James Nachtwey, Photographer

Silver

The New York Times Magazine

Janet Froelich, Art Director; Kathi Rota, Designer; Kandy Littrell, Designer; Kathy Ryan, Photo Editor; Josef Astor, Photographer; John Collier, Illustrator; David Sandlin, Illustrator; Ross MacDonald, Illustrator; Gary Panter, Illustrator; Anthony Russo, Illustrator

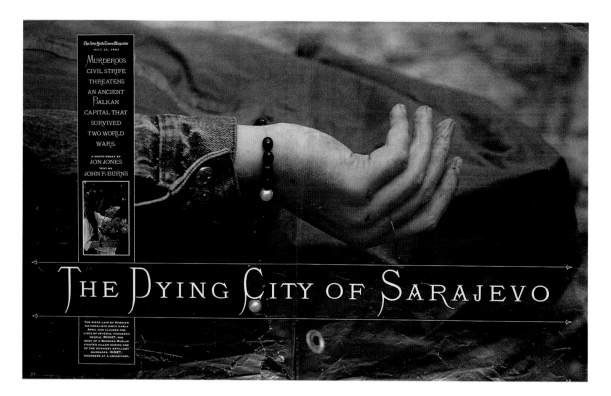

Silver

The New York Times Magazine

Janet Froelich, Art Director; Kandy Littrell, Designer; Kathy Ryan, Photo Editor; Jon Jones, Photographer

Bronze
The New York Times Magazine

Janet Froelich, Art Director; Kandy Littrell, Designer; Kathy Ryan, Photo Editor; Michael O'Brien, Photographer

Bronze
The Washington Post Magazine

Kelly Doe, Art Director & Designer; David Hughes, Illustrator

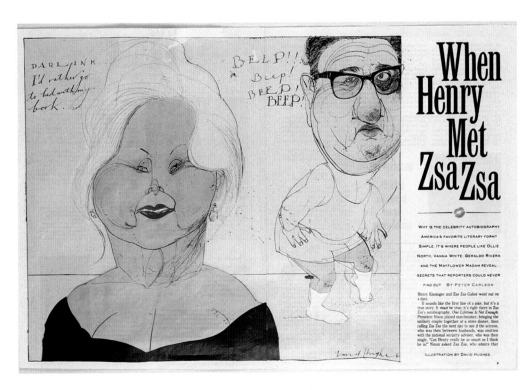

Bronze

San Francisco Examiner

Josephine Rigg, Art Director; Zahid Sardar, Associate Art Director; Penni Gladstone, Picture Editor

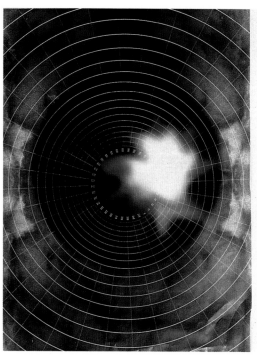

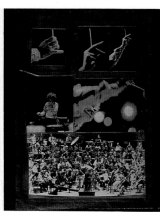

Award of Excellence

The New York Times Magazine

Janet Froelich, Art Director; Kathi Rota, Designer; Kathy Ryan, Photo Editor; Douglas Brothers Photographers

Award of Excellence

The Washington Post Magazine

Richard Baker, Art Director & Designer; Deborah Needleman, Photo Editor; Frank Ockenfels, Photographer

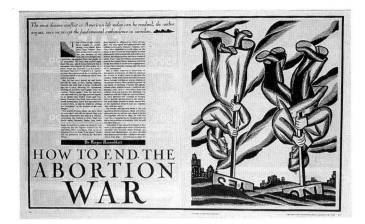

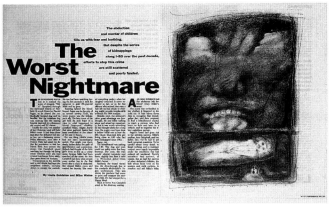

Award of Excellence

El Mundo/El Periodico de Cataluna

Madrid, Spain

Jeff Goertzen, Art Director; Andrew Lucas, Illustrator; Karl Gude,
Infographic Editor; Mario Tascon, Infographic Editor; Xavier Conesa,
Infographic Editor; Roberto Dominguez, Infographic Editor; El Mundo
Staff; El Periodico Staff

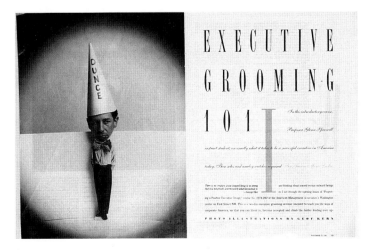

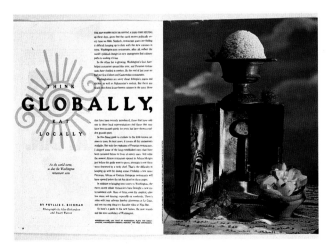

Award of Excellence

The Washington Post Magazine

Richard Baker, Art Director & Designer; Deborah
Needleman, Photo Editor; Geof Kern, Photo Illustrator

Award of Excellence

The Washington Post Magazine

Richard Baker, Art Director & Designer; Karen Tanaka, Photo Editor; Alan Richardson,
Photographer

Bronze

Barcelona '92

Pamplona, Spain

Ricardo Bermejo, Design/Art Direction (BEGA); Luis Garbayo, News Editor/Design (BEGA); Guillermo Nagore, Design Editor; Rafa Esquiroz, Designer (BEGA); Juancho Cruz, Layout Staff; Eduardo Cruz, Layout Staff; Pablo Lopez, Layout Staff; Fernando Lopez Urdin, Layout Staff; Roser de Manuel-Rimbau, Layout Staff; Anna Nogue, Layout Staff

Bronze

The Atlanta Journal/Constitution

Tony De Feria, Section Designer & Art Director; Peter Dishal, Daily Designer; Robert Mashburn, Daily Designer; Thomas Oliver, Editor; Glenn Hannigan, Editor; John Walter, Editor; Art Staff & Illustrators; Mike Gordon, Design Director

Award of Excellence
La Vanguardia
Barcelona, Spain

Carlos Perez de Rozas, Art Director; Rosa Mundet, Assistant Art Director; Pepe Baeza, Photo Editor; Jose Alberola; Design Editor; Jordi Paris, Graphics Editor; Ferran Grau, Designer; Emili Alvarez, Designer; Angels Soler, Designer

Award of Excellence
Saint Paul Pioneer Press
St. Paul, MN

Don Wyatt, Executive News Editor; Nancy Ward, Graphics Coordinator; Tim Van Ness, Graphics Artist; Richard Marshall, Photographer; Nancy Conner, Metro Graphics Coordinator; Jeff Sjerven, Copy Editor

Award of Excellence
Saint Paul Pioneer Press
St. Paul, MN

Stacy Sweat, Art Director; Nancy Ward, Graphics Coordinator; Laura Hopple Treston, Page Designer; Bill Bradley, Page Layout; Staff Artists & Photographers

Award of Excellence
The Sun
Bremerton, WA

Scott Whitcomb, Designer

Award of Excellence
The Christian Science Monitor

John Van Pelt, Design Director; Melanie Stetson Freeman, Photo Editor; Karen Everbeck, Page Designer; Shirely Horn, Graphic Art; R. Norman Matheny, Photographer; Ann S. Tyson, Photographer

Award of Excellence
Daily Republic

Fairfield, CA

Colleen Lanchester, Designer; Mona Reeder, Photographer

Award of Excellence
El Mundo

Madrid, Spain

Carmelo Caderot, Art Director & Designer; Manuel de Miguel, Assistant Art Director; Ricardo Martinez, Illustrator

Award of Excellence
Detroit Free Press

Deborah Withey, Design Director & Designer; Robert Pizzo, Illustrator; Wayne Kamidoi, Designer

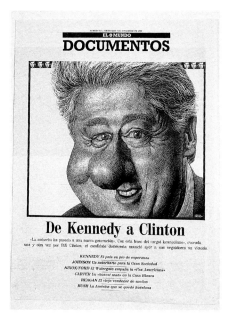

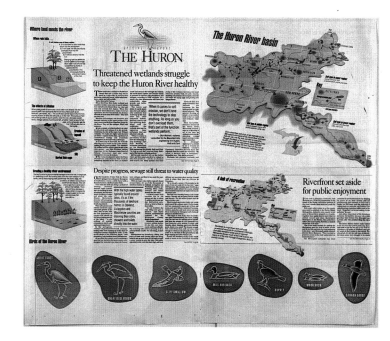

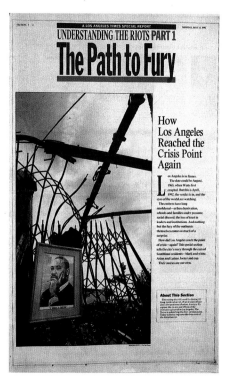

Award of Excellence
The Ann Arbor News

Ann Arbor, MI

Karl Leif Bates, Staff Reporter; Alan Bliss, News Art Director

Award of Excellence
Los Angeles Times

Staff

Award of Excellence
The New York Times

Fred Norgaard, Art Director & Designer; Megan Jaegerman, Graphics Artist; Bedel Saget, Graphics Artist; Seth Feaster, Graphics Artist; Al Granberg, Graphics Artist; John Papasian, Graphics Artist; Rosendo Toro, Graphics Artist; Tom Bodkin, Design Director; Rich Meislin, Graphics Editor

Award of Excellence
The Sacramento Bee

Sacramento, CA

Lisa Roberts, Graphics Editor

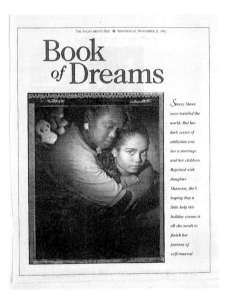

Award of Excellence
Detroit Free Press

Steve Anderson, Designer; George Waldman, Photographer

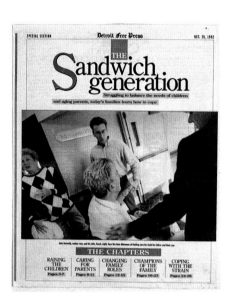

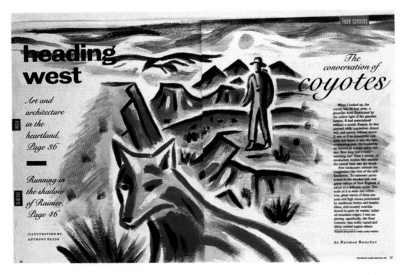

Award of Excellence
The Boston Globe Magazine

Rena Sokolow, Art Director; Jacqueline Berthet, Photo Researcher; Ward Schumaker, Illustrations & Maps; Anthony Russo, Illustrator; Rollin McGrail, Illustrator

Award of Excellence
El Pais

Madrid, Spain

Manuel M. Fuentes, Designer

Award of Excellence

The Wall Street Journal Reports

Greg Leeds, Designer & Design Director; Nick Klein, Designer

Award of Excellence

The News Journal

Wilmington, DE

Staff

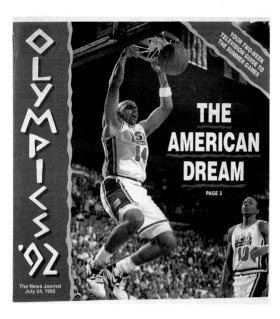

Award of Excellence

El Mundo

Madrid, Spain

Ricardo Martinez, Illustrator & Designer

Award of Excellence

Anchorage Daily News

Galie Jean-Louis, Features Design Director & Designer; Scott Menchin, Illustrator

Award of Excellence

Saint Paul Pioneer Press

St. Paul, MN

Stacy Sweat, Art Director & Designer; Bill Alkofer, Photographer; Janet Hostetter, Color Lab Technician

Bronze

The Detroit News

Nancy Hanus, Assistant News Editor; Felecia Henderson, Copy Editor/Designer; Dale Peskin, Assistant Managing Editor

Award of Excellence

The Patriot Ledger

Quincy, MA

Dorene Reardon, Designer

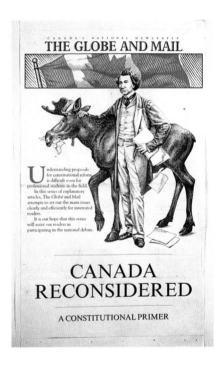

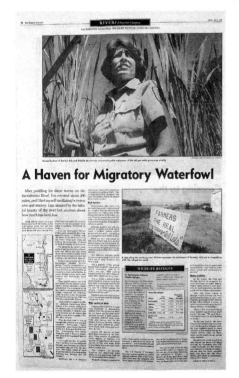

Bronze

The Globe and Mail

Toronto, Canada

Michael Gregg, Design Director; Gordon Sauve, Illustrator; Michael Valpy, Editor

Award of Excellence

San Francisco Chronicle

Dorothy Yule, Designer; Hulda Nelson, Art Director; Steve Outing, Graphics Editor; Bruce Krefting, Graphic Artist; Alyx Meltzer, Graphics Researcher; Gary Fong, Photo Director

Gold
The Detroit News
Dale Peskin, AME

War zone

Rage in L.A.

Highlights

■ **Help sought:** Los Angeles and California officials asked federal authorities to put U.S. military forces on standby alert.

■ **Bush:** President met with aides in the Oval Office to consider the request for military help.

■ **Troops:** The National Guard force in Los Angeles may be increased to 6,000 from 4,000.

■ **Rage:** Violent protest in Atlanta; state of emergency in San Francisco, where 900 are arrested; riots surge over California.

■ **White House reacts:** President condemned the widespread rioting as "ugly mob brutality." He meets today with nation's black leaders.

Inside

■ **Painful lesson:** Local students shocked. Page 1B

■ **Your views:** Readers react to King verdict. Page 2B

■ **Pepper:** Life will be worse after riot. Page 1E

■ **Editorial:** L.A. law needs review. Page 10A

■ **More coverage:** Pages 6-8A

DAVID LONGSTREATH/Associated Press

National Guard troops backed up thousands of police officers in Los Angeles Thursday.

■ **No end:** Bush considers putting U.S. military forces on standby alert. Los Angeles mayor requests 2,000 more National Guard troops, too.

DETROIT NEWS WIRE SERVICES

LOS ANGELES — After a second night of looting and destruction, city and state officials today asked federal authorities to put U.S. military forces on standby alert and requested that 2,000 more National Guard troops be deployed in Los Angeles County.

In Washington, President Bush summoned top administration officials to the White House today to consider the request. Bush met in the Oval Office with Gen. Colin Powell, chairman of the Joint Chiefs of Staff, FBI Director William Sessions and Defense Department officials to assess the situation in California, which was described as "explosive" by Health and Human Services Secretary Louis Sullivan.

In appealing to Washington for help, California Gov. Pete Wilson said, "We are determined that this city is not going to suffer the kind of terrorism that some people seem bent on inflicting."

Los Angeles Mayor Tom Bradley, appearing with Wilson at an early morning news conference, admitted that "it is clear now that we need more than" the 4,000 Guardsmen already on the streets.

By 7 a.m. today (4 a.m. Los Angeles time) at least 27 people had been killed, about 900 injured and 400 arrested in the Los Angeles area. Fire damage alone was put at more than $200 million.

But the violence was spreading far beyond Los Angeles County.

Rioting triggered by the acquittal of four policemen charged in the beating of Rodney King hit Atlanta, more than 2,000 miles away. There were disturbances as well in Las Vegas, Seattle and Eugene, Ore. Trouble also swept other California cities, engulfing downtown San Francisco — where 900 people were reported arrested — and claiming lives in San Bernardino and Long Beach. Looting reached even into Hollywood and Beverly Hills.

Earlier Bush, speaking at a $1,000-a-plate campaign dinner, condemned the widespread rioting as "ugly mob

Please see War, 8A

RODNEY KING

'Why? Why? Why?...Why are they beating me again?'

By Richard A. Serrano
LOS ANGELES TIMES

LOS ANGELES — The not guilty verdicts left Rodney King stunned, speechless and shaking.

On the television screen, the four Los Angeles police officers accused of beating him had just been found innocent. They were hugging and smiling in the courtroom.

But King, the 26-year-old motorist whose life took a dramatic turn on a midnight drive in the San Fernando Valley 14 months ago, locked himself inside his bedroom.

According to recollections Thursday from relatives, friends and members of King's growing legal entourage, his occasional shouts could be heard through the doorjamb:

"Why? Why? Why?" he reportedly cried. "Why are they beating me again?"

As night came, and rioters and looters spread mayhem on city streets, a psychiatrist was called in. The therapist administered an antidepressant drug and tried to coax King out of his sinking state.

The doctor, who spent four hours with King Wednesday night, said King is extremely angry he was never called to the witness stand during the officers' trial.

He is confused and bewildered about the rioting sparked by the verdicts — during which his name frequently is chanted. But he is afraid to speak out publicly against the upheaval, fearful that his words might be misinterpreted and only further ignite the protests.

He is upset that his personal

Please see King, 5A

'What good are they doing by looting and burning everything?'

LOS ANGELES — There was an awful stench in the air, and it was more than the foul aroma of burning rubber and charred wood.

The City of Angels had become a violent war zone of misplaced anger and frustration. This was a city amok in reaction to the verdict that acquitted four Los Angeles police officers of the savage beating of black motorist Rodney King.

Thick, black clouds of smoke billowed out of the remains of liquor stores and stereo shops and fast-food joints and auto repair garages. Stores that weren't burning were being scavenged by looters. They were crawling out of the broken windows of The Boys' Market in southwest L.A., carrying overstuffed bags and boxes of food. A block away, even as an

alarm siren wailed, four teen-agers squeezed through the metal bars of a stereo shop, racing away — empty-handed — from an unmarked police car loaded with shotgun-toting undercover cops.

Down the block, in front of the Avenue Barber Shop on Manchester Avenue, Isaac Burton sat on the steps of his shop

Please see Burwell, 5A

BRYAN BURWELL

Cheveldae shines in Wings 5-2 win

■ **Chicago next:** Detroit goalie makes 29 saves to shut down Minnesota. Wings host Chicago Saturday at Joe Louis Arena in the Norris Division finals. Page 1C

Traxler quits House seat Page 3A

■ **Loss of power:** Congressman becomes 5th from Michigan this year to retire.

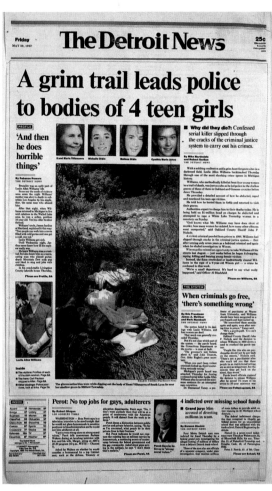

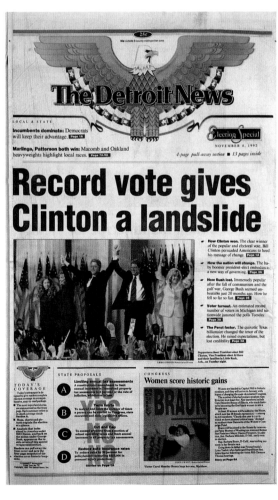

Gold

The Miami Herald

Ana Lense-Larrauri, Illustrator & Designer; Jim Watters, Business Monday News Editor; Rex Seline, Executive Business Editor; Randy Stano, Director/Editorial Art & Design

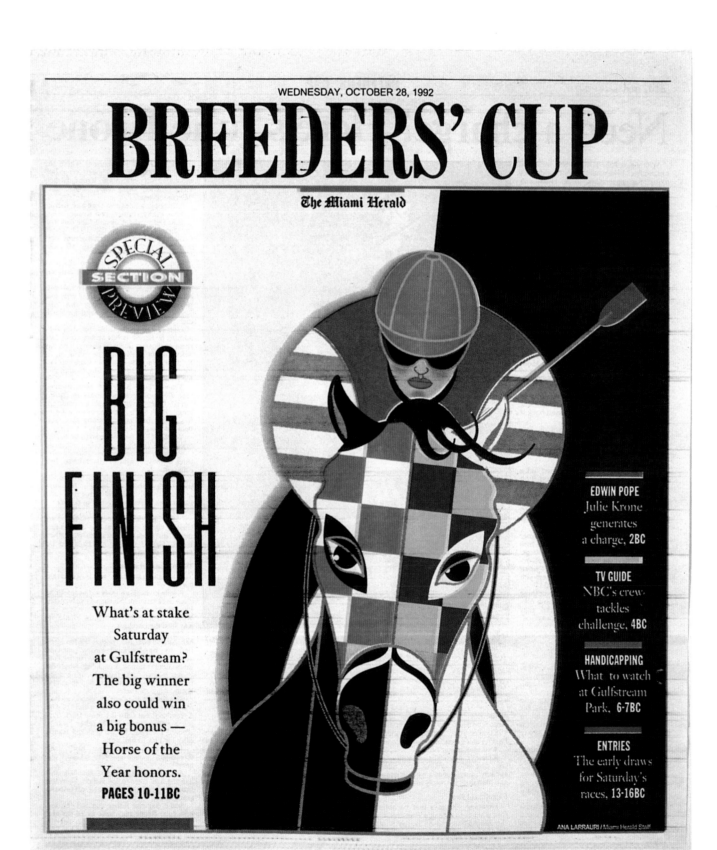

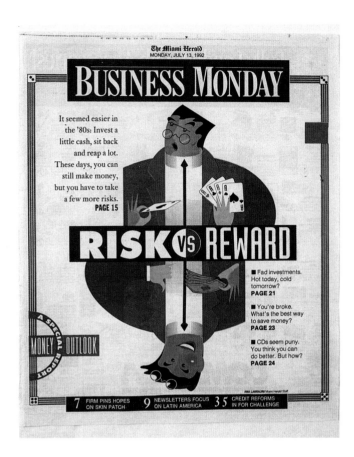

The Miami Herald
MONDAY, JULY 13, 1992

BUSINESS MONDAY

It seemed easier in the '80s: Invest a little cash, sit back and reap a lot. These days, you can still make money, but you have to take a few more risks.
PAGE 15

RISK vs REWARD

■ Fad investments. Hot today, cold tomorrow?
PAGE 21

■ You're broke. What's the best way to save money?
PAGE 23

■ CDs seem puny. You think you can do better. But how?
PAGE 24

A SPECIAL REPORT
MONEY OUTLOOK

ANA LARRAURI Miami Herald Staff

7 FIRM PINS HOPES ON SKIN PATCH **9** NEWSLETTERS FOCUS ON LATIN AMERICA **35** CREDIT REFORMS IN FOR CHALLENGE

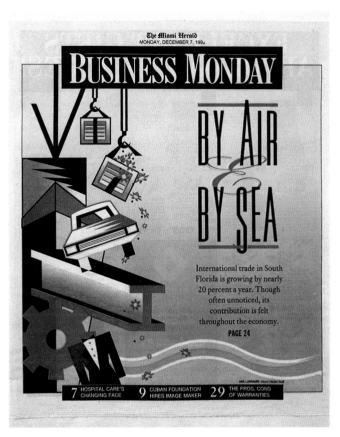

The Miami Herald
MONDAY, DECEMBER 7, 1992

BUSINESS MONDAY

BY AIR & BY SEA

International trade in South Florida is growing by nearly 20 percent a year. Though often unnoticed, its contribution is felt throughout the economy.
PAGE 24

ANA LARRAURI Miami Herald Staff

7 HOSPITAL CARE'S CHANGING FACE **9** CUBAN FOUNDATION HIRES IMAGE MAKER **29** THE PROS, CONS OF WARRANTIES

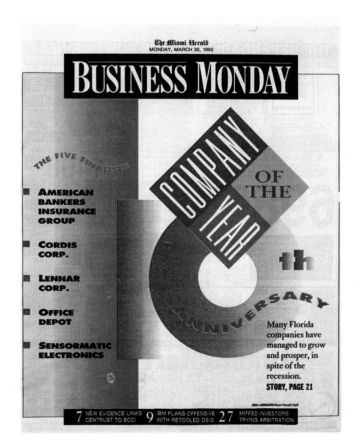

The Miami Herald
MONDAY, MARCH 30, 1992

BUSINESS MONDAY

THE FIVE FINALISTS

■ **AMERICAN BANKERS INSURANCE GROUP**

■ **CORDIS CORP.**

■ **LENNAR CORP.**

■ **OFFICE DEPOT**

■ **SENSORMATIC ELECTRONICS**

COMPANY OF THE YEAR

8th ANNIVERSARY

Many Florida companies have managed to grow and prosper, in spite of the recession.
STORY, PAGE 21

ANA LARRAURI Miami Herald Staff

7 NEW EVIDENCE LINKS CENTRUST TO BCCI **9** IBM PLANS OFFENSIVE WITH RETOOLED OS/2 **27** MIFFED INVESTORS TRYING ARBITRATION

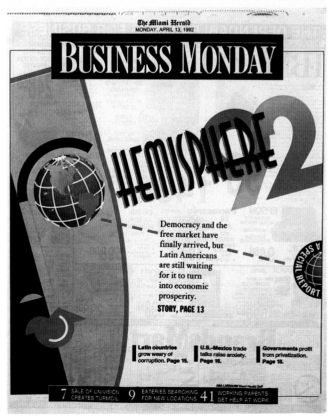

The Miami Herald
MONDAY, APRIL 13, 1992

BUSINESS MONDAY

HEMISPHERE 92

Democracy and the free market have finally arrived, but Latin Americans are still waiting for it to turn into economic prosperity.
STORY, PAGE 13

A SPECIAL REPORT

■ Latin countries grow weary of corruption. Page 15.

■ U.S.-Mexico trade talks raise anxiety. Page 16.

■ Governments profit from privatization. Page 18.

ANA LARRAURI Miami Herald Staff

7 SALE OF UNIVISION CREATES TURMOIL **9** EATERIES SEARCHING FOR NEW LOCATIONS **41** WORKING PARENTS GET HELP AT WORK

Bronze

Dagens Nyheter

Stockholm, Sweden

Thomas Hall, Designer

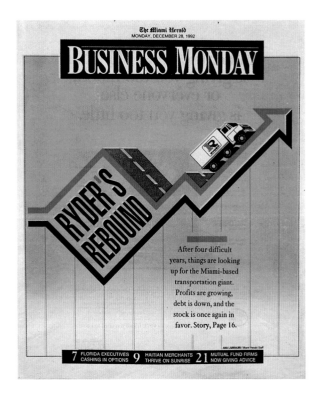

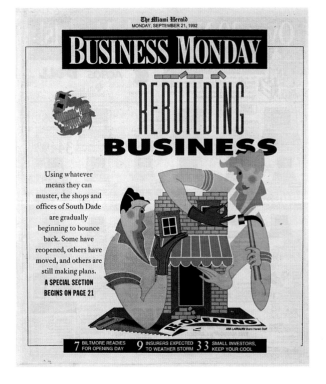

Bronze

The Miami Herald

Ana Lense-Larrauri, Illustrator & Designer; Jim Watters, Business Monday News Editor;
Rex Seline, Executive Business Editor; Randy Stano, Director/Editorial Art & Design

Award of Excellence

Los Angeles Times

Paul Gonzales, Art Director & Designer

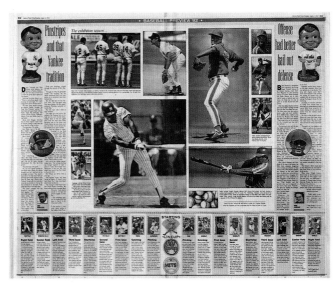

Award of Excellence

Asbury Park Press

Neptune, NJ

Tim Oliver, Page Designer

Silver

The Washington Times

Paul Compton, Art Director & Designer

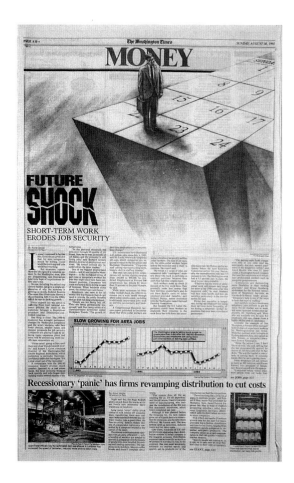

Award of Excellence

Gazette Telegraph

Colorado Springs, CO

Tim Filby, Designer

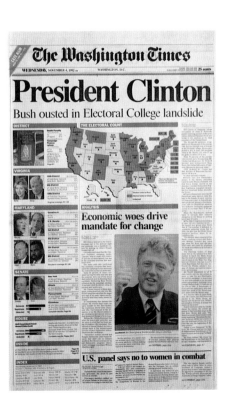

Award of Excellence
The Washington Times
George Kolb, Sports Layout Editor

Award of Excellence
Anchorage Daily News
Mike Campbell, AME Graphics

Award of Excellence
The Sunday Tribune
Dublin, Ireland
Stephen Ryan, Editor & Designer; Paul Hipkins,
Production Editor

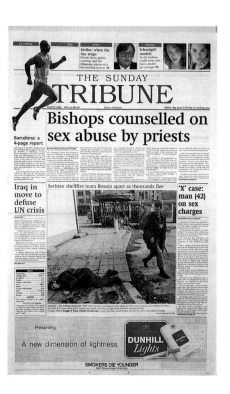

Bronze

The Albuquerque Tribune

Lara Edge, Designer

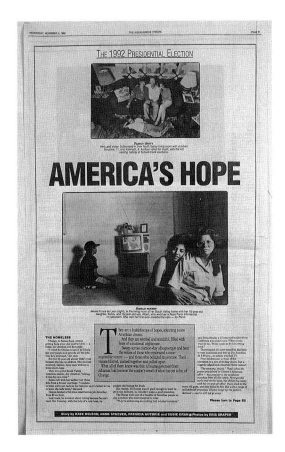

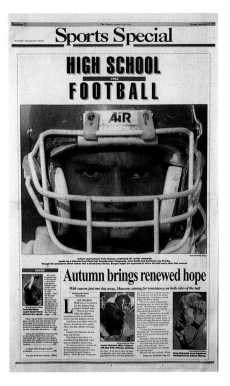

Award of Excellence

The Citizen

Auburn, NY

Gary Piccirillo, AME Design

Silver & JSR

The New York Times

Ken McFarlin, Art Director & Designer

Silver

The Boston Globe

Cynthia Daniels, Art Director

Silver

The Boston Globe

Rena Sokolow, Art Director & Designer; Scott Menchin, Illustrator;
Gary Baseman, Illustrator; FPG International Photos; Bill Mayer,
Illustrator; Kurt Vargo, Illustrator; Scott McKowen, Illustrator

Award of Excellence

Detroit Free Press

Keith Webb, Art Director & Designer

Bronze

The Charlotte Observer

Charlotte, NC

Sarah Blaydon, Designer

Award of Excellence

The Globe and Mail

Toronto, Canada

Eric Nelson, Art Director & Designer; Sarah Murdoch, Editor

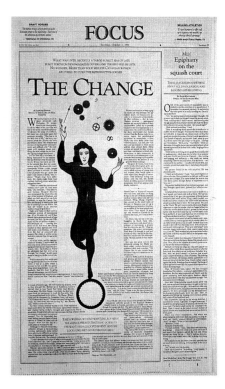

Bronze

The Wall Street Journal Reports

Greg Leeds, Designer & Design Director

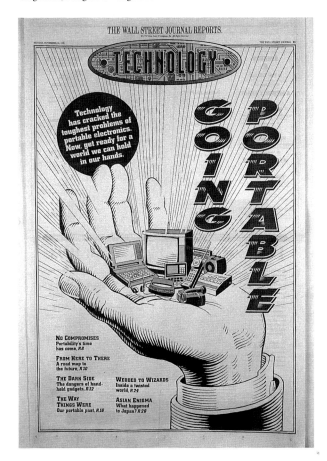

Award of Excellence

The Miami Herald

Herman Vega, Designer; Rhonda Prast, Features
Design Editor

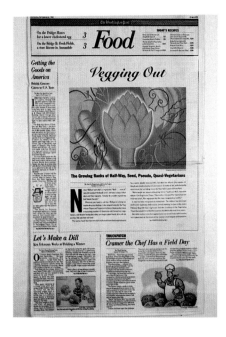

Silver

El Mundo

Madrid, Spain

Carmelo Caderot, Art Director & Designer; Manuel de Miguel,
Assistant Art Director

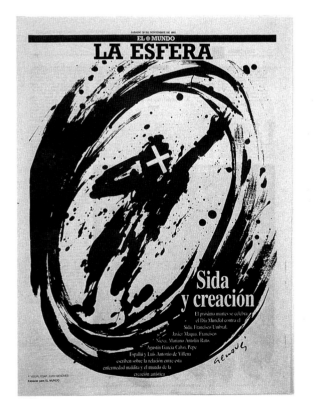

Bronze

El Mundo

Madrid, Spain

Carmelo Caderot, Art Director & Designer; Manuel de Miguel,
Assistant Art Director

Silver

El Norte

Monterrey, Mexico

Carmen A. Escobedo, Designer

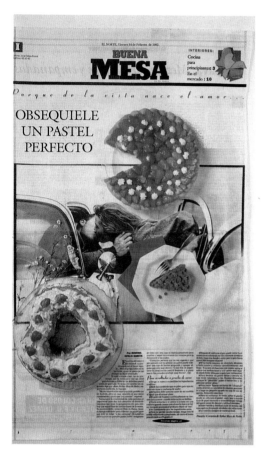

Silver

El Nuevo Herald

Miami, FL

Rosa Bautista, Editor; Raul
Fernandez, Illustrator & Designer;
Nuri Ducassi, Art Director

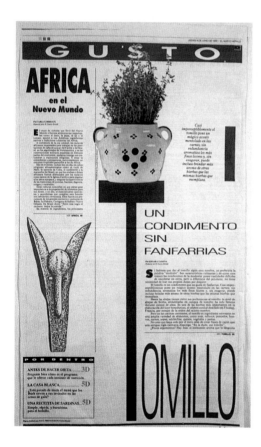

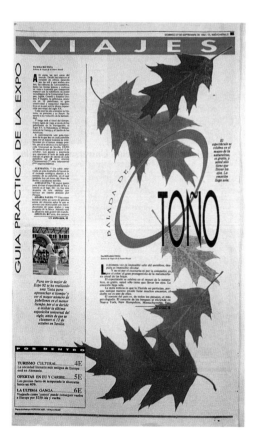

Silver

The Washington Times

David B. Bartlett, Art Director

Silver

San Francisco Examiner

Don McCartney, Designer; Kelly Frankeny, Art Director

Bronze

El Nuevo Herald

Miami, FL

Nuri Ducassi, Art Director, Designer & Illustrator

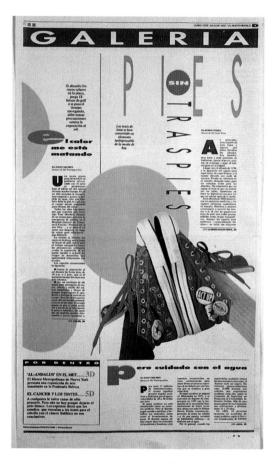

Bronze

New Times

Phoenix, AZ

Brian Stauffer, Art Director; Timothy Archibald, Photographer; Steve Brodner, Illustrator

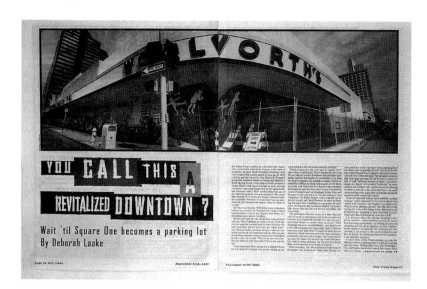

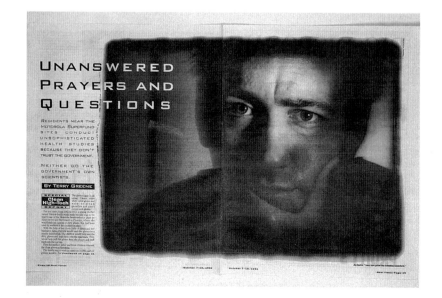

Bronze

El Nuevo Herald

Miami, FL

Nuri Ducassi, Art Director & Designer

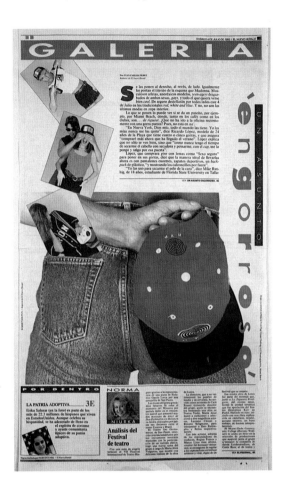

Award of Excellence

El Nuevo Herald

Miami, FL

Aurora Arrue, Illustrator & Designer; Nuri Ducassi, Art Director; Silvia Licha, Editor

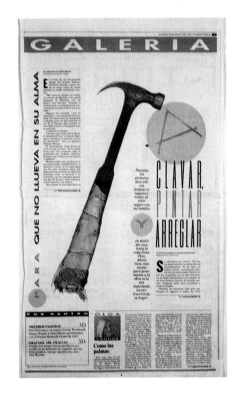

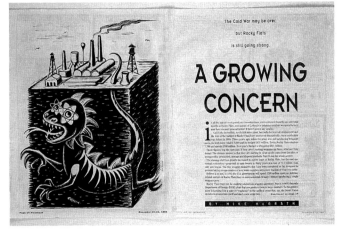

Bronze

Westword

Denver, CO

Kat Allen, Art Director

Silver

Anchorage Daily News

Galie Jean-Louis, Features Design Director; Dee Boyles,
Features Designer/Illustrator

Bronze

Houston Press

Audrey Satterwhite, Art Director; Ted Keller, Assistant Art
Director; John Wilburn, Editor; Pam Francis, Photographer

Award of Excellence

Anchorage Daily News

Galie Jean-Louis, Features Design Director; Pamela
Dunlap-Shohl, Features Designer; Lin Mitchell,
Photographer; Joy Rodgers, Copy Editor; Galie Jean-
Louis, Photo Editor

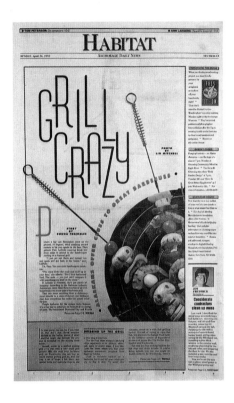

Award of Excellence

The Albuquerque Tribune

Annemarie Neff, Designer

Bronze

The UCSD Guardian

La Jolla, CA

James Collier, Designer & Design Editor; Mel Marcelo, Graphics Editor

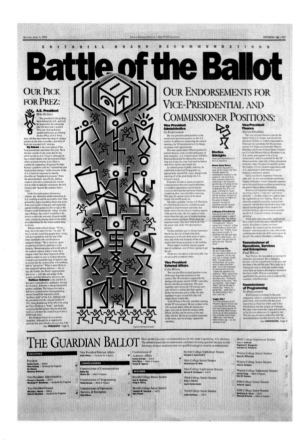

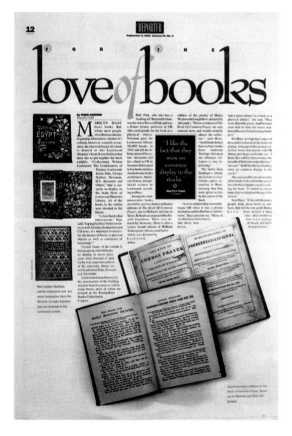

Bronze

Reporter

Buffalo, NY

Rebecca Farnham, Art Director

Gold

Eastsideweek

Kirkland, WA

Sandra Schneider, Art Director; Saul Bromberger, Photographer; Sandra Hoover, Photographer; Tina Fong, Illustrator; Jerry Gay, Photographer; Karen Moskowitz, Photographer; Mark Van-S, Photographer

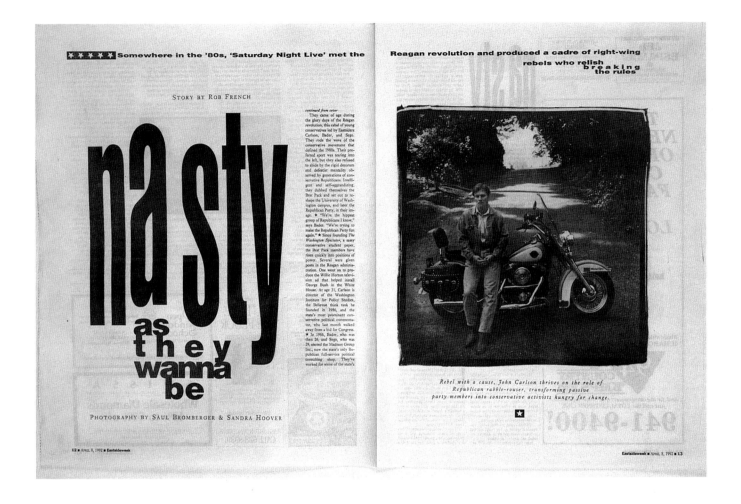

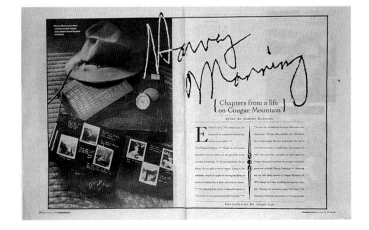

Silver

The Boston Globe

Lucy Bartholomay, Art Director & Designer; Anita Kunz, Illustrator; James Yang, Illustrator; Michele McDonald, Photographer; Scott Menchin, Illustrator; Allan Frederickson, Photographer; Reuter Photographer

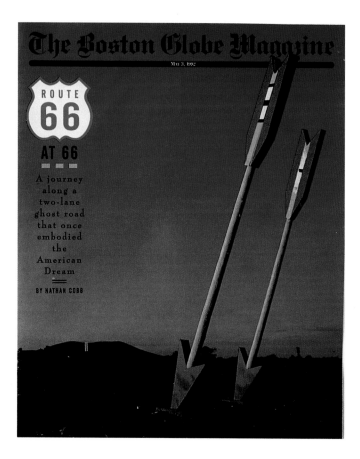

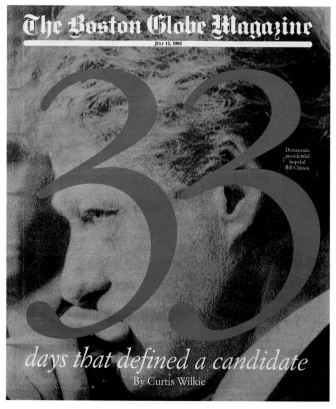

Award of Excellence
The Washington Post Magazine

Richard Baker, Art Director; Kelly Doe, Deputy Art Director/Designer; Janet Woolley, Illustrator; Jennifer Bishop, Photographer; Deborah Needleman, Photo Editor; Brian Ajar, Illustrator; David Hughes, Illustrator; Steve Szabo, Photographer; Karen Tanaka; Photo Editor; Brian Smale, Photographer

Award of Excellence
The Santa Fe New Mexican

Santa Fe, NM

Mel Nathanson, Graphics Designer

Award of Excellence
The San Francisco Bay Guardian
Tracy Cox, Art Director & Designer; David Gifford, Illustrator

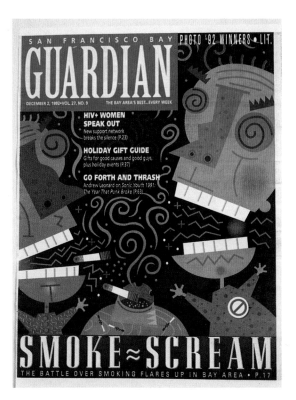

Award of Excellence
The Press-Enterprise
Riverside, CA
Stephen Sedam-Stone, Artist & Designer

Award of Excellence

The Hartford Courant

Hartford, CT

Patti Nelson, Designer & Design Director; Stephen
Dunn, Photographer; Scott Menchin, Illustrator;
Michael McAndrews, Photographer

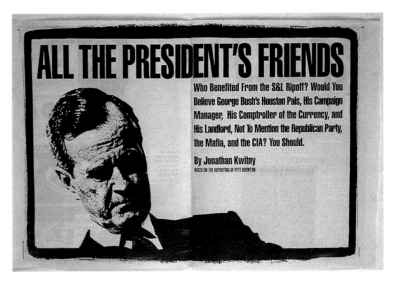

Award of Excellence

The Village Voice

Robert Newman, Design Director; Florian Bachveda,
Designer

Gold

The Daily Breeze

Torrance, CA

Robert E. Clark, Photographer; Jeannie Grand, Graphics
Editor; Lisa Reitzel, AME

Silver
The Detroit News
Joe DeVera, Photographer

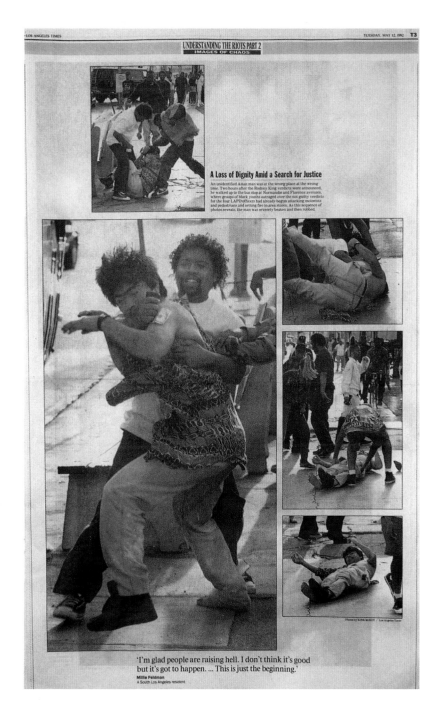

Bronze
Los Angeles Times
Kirk McKoy, Photographer

Bronze

The Spokesman-Review

Spokane, WA

Colin Mulvany, Photographer

Award of Excellence

Dagens Nyheter

Stockholm, Sweden

Sven-Erik Sjoberg, Photographer

Award of Excellence

The Citizen

Auburn, NY

Kevin Rivoli, Photo Editor

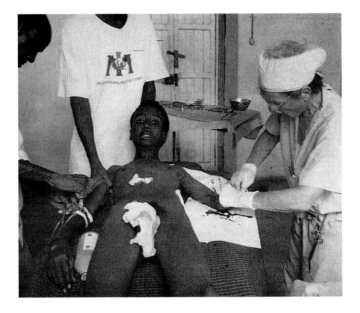

Award of Excellence
The Houston Chronicle
Paul S. Howell, Photographer

Award of Excellence
Los Angeles Daily News
Woodland Hills, CA
Kim Kulish, Photographer; Craig Mailloux,
Photographer

Award of Excellence
Los Angeles Times

Rosemary Kaul, Photographer; Alan Duignan,
Photographer; Pat Downs, Photographer

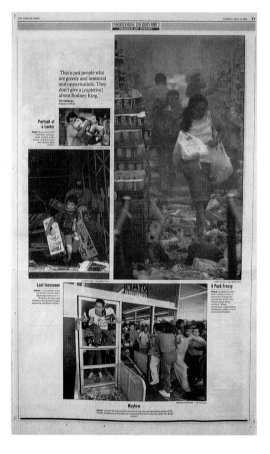

Award of Excellence
Los Angeles Times

Hyungwon Kang, Photographer; Kirk McCoy, Photographer; Mike
Meadows, Photographer; Larry Davis, Photographer

Award of Excellence
Los Angeles Times

Larry Davis, Photographer; J. Albert Diaz, Photographer; Gerard
Burkhart, Photographer

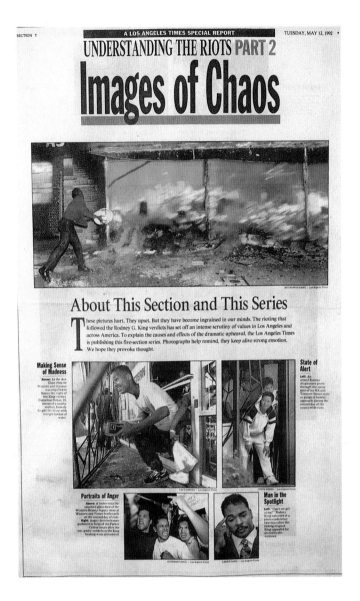

Award of Excellence
Los Angeles Times
Hyungwon Kang, Photographer; Lacy Atkins, Photographer;
Steve Dykes, Photographer; Rosemary Kaul, Photographer;
Larry Davis, Photographer

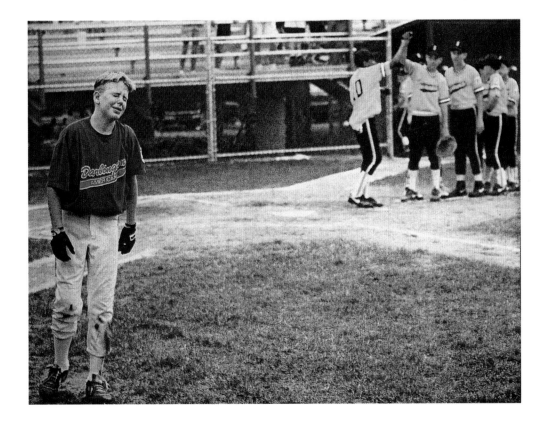

Award of Excellence
*The Providence
Journal-Bulletin*
Providence, RI
Timothy Barmann, Photographer

Award of Excellence
The Boston Globe
Michele McDonald, Photographer; Lucy
Bartholomay, Art Director

Award of Excellence
Concord Monitor
Concord, NH
Dan Habib, Former Staff Photographer

Award of Excellence
The New York Times Magazine
Nigel Parry, Photographer; Kathy Ryan, Photo Editor;
Janet Froelich, Art Director; Richard Samperi, Designer

Award of Excellence
The Milwaukee Journal
Dale Guldan, Photographer

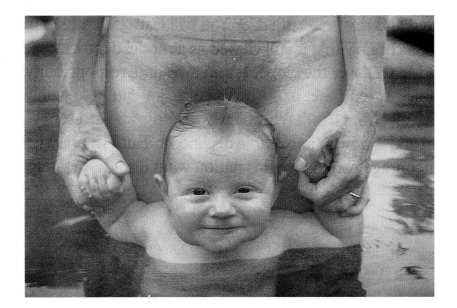

Award of Excellence
The Philadelphia Inquirer Magazine
Nicholas DeVore III, Photographer; Bert Fox, Photo Editor &
Art Director; Jessica Helfand, Design Director; Karen Heller,
Writer

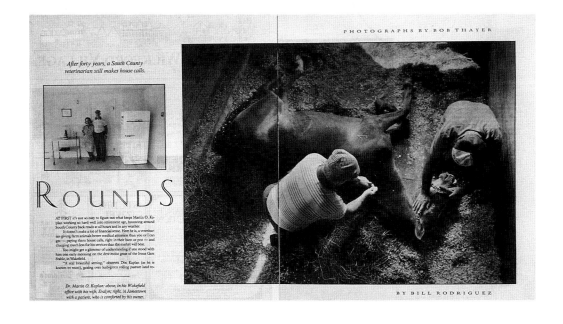

Award of Excellence
*The Providence
Journal-Bulletin*
Providence, RI
Bob Thayer, Photographer

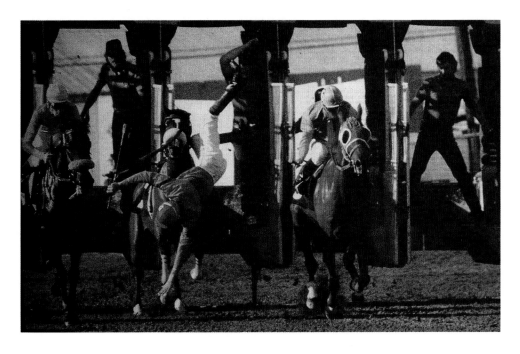

Award of Excellence
The Spokesman-Review
Spokane, WA
Colin Mulvany, Photographer

Silver (also an Award of Excellence for Design)
The New York Times Magazine
Andrew Eccles, Photographer; Kathy Ryan, Photo Editor;
Janet Froelich, Art Director; Kandy Littrell, Designer

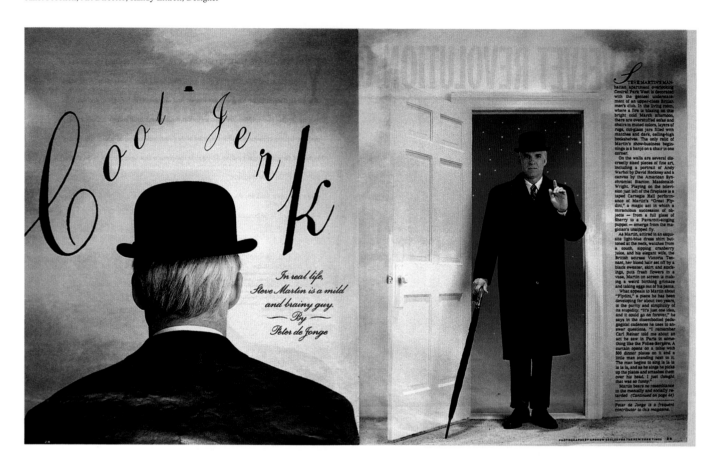

Silver
The Hartford Courant
Hartford, CT
Brad Clift, Photographer; Randy Cox, Designer

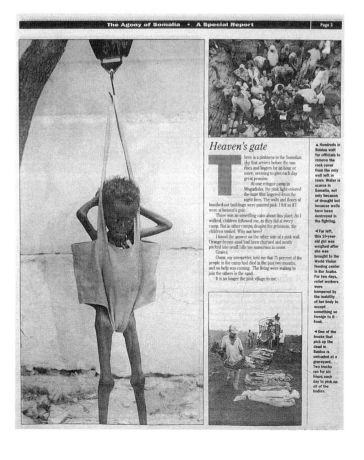

Silver

Journal Star

Peoria, IL

Fred Zwicky, Photographer; John Kaplan, Photo Editor;
Christine McNeal, AME Graphics/Photography

Before he Leaves

Nineteen-year-old John Keets believes it is his duty to
educate the public about AIDS, the disease that is stealing
his life. This is the story of his mission, and of the small
Midwestern town that has embraced it.

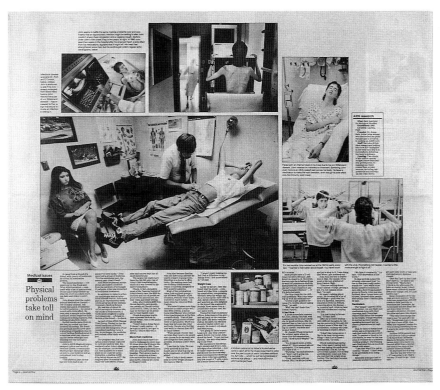

Physical problems take toll on mind

Silver

Monterey Herald

Monterey, CA

John Kaplan,
Designer/Photographer

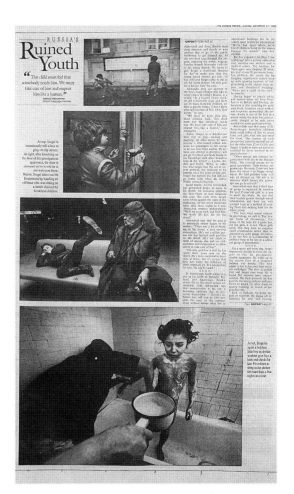

RUSSIA'S Ruined Youth

" This child must feel that
somebody needs him. We must
take care of him and respect
him like a human. "

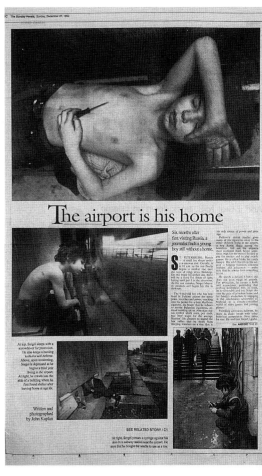

The airport is his home

Six months after
first visiting Russia, a
journalist finds a young
boy still without a home.

Written and
photographed
by John Kaplan

Bronze

Los Angeles Times

Staff Photographers

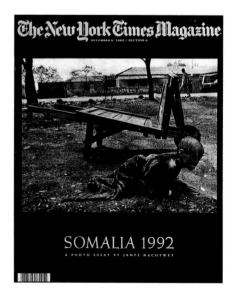

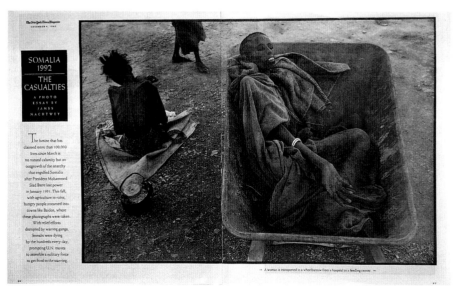

Bronze

The New York Times Magazine

James Nachtwey, Photographer; Kathy Ryan, Photo
Editor; Janet Froelich, Art Director & Designer

Award of Excellence

La Vanguardia

Barcelona, Spain

Kim Manresa, Photographer; Pepe Baeza, Photo Editor;
Guillermina Puig, Photo Editor; Carlos Perez de Rozas,
Art Director

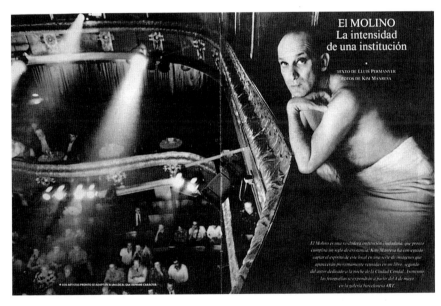

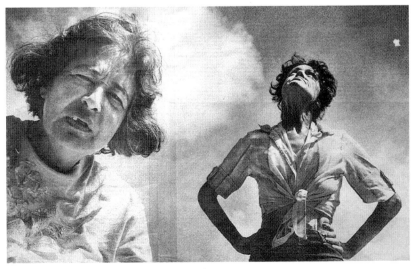

Gold

El Pais Semanal

Madrid, Spain

Manuel Zambrana, Photographer; Almudena Solana, Writer; Eugenio Gonzalez, Design Director; Isabel Benito, Designer; Gustavo Sanchez, Designer; Marta Calzada, Designer

Silver

The New York Times

Michelle Clement, Photographer; Janet Froelich, Art Director; Kathi Rota, Designer

 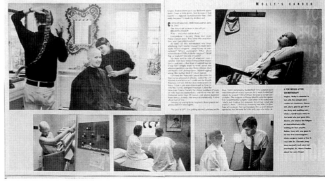

Bronze

The Seattle Times

Betty Udesen, Photographer; Gary Settle, Photo Editor; Robin Avni, Art Director & Designer

Award of Excellence
Lexington Herald-Leader
Lexington, KY
Charles Bertram, Photographer; Jim Jennings,
AME/Graphics

Award of Excellence
Los Angeles Times
Larry Armstrong, Photo Director; Con Keyes, Picture Editor; Michael Edwards, Picture Editor; Lily Dow Kuroda,
Designer; Tom Trapnell, Designer

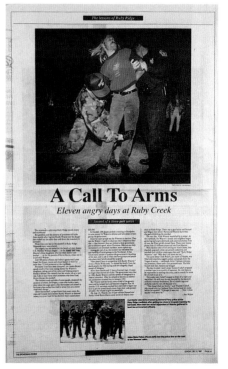

Award of Excellence
The Seattle Times
Harley Soltes, Photographer; Gary Settle, Photo Editor; Robin Avni, Art Director, Designer & Photo Editor

Award of Excellence
The Spokesman-Review
Spokane, WA
Scott Sines, AME/Visual; Photo Staff; Jim Allen,
Sunday Editor

Award of Excellence
The Topeka Capital-Journal
Topeka, KS
David Eulitt, Photographer

Award of Excellence
The Village Voice
Lois Green, Photographer; Tom McGovern, Photo Editor; Robert Newman, Design Director; Kate Thompson, Designer

Silver
San Jose Mercury News
Paul Kitagaki Jr., Photographer

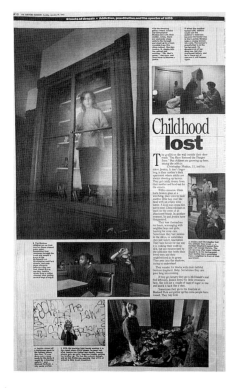

Award of Excellence
The Hartford Courant
Hartford, CT
Brad Clift, Photographer

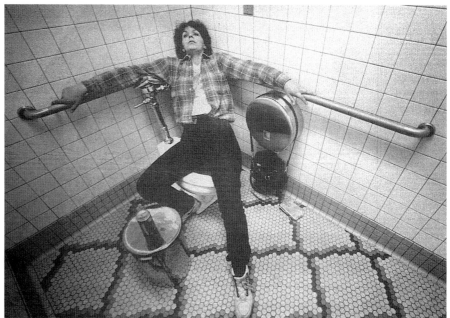

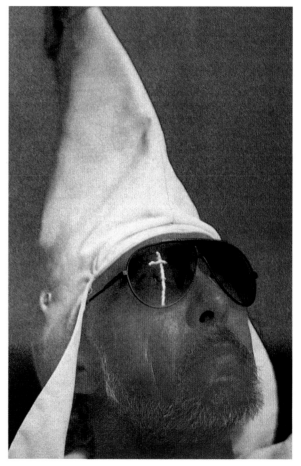

Award of Excellence
The Houston Chronicle
Howard Castleberry, Photographer

Award of Excellence
The Sacramento Bee
Sacramento, CA
Jose Luis Villegas, Photographer

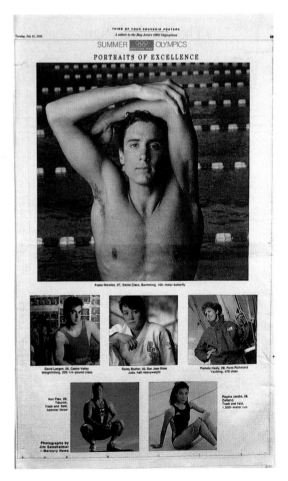

Award of Excellence
San Jose Mercury News
Jim Gensheimer, Photographer; Sue Morrow, Designer

Bronze

The Providence Sunday Journal

Providence, RI

Bob Thayer, Photographer; Anestis Diakopoulos, Photo Editor; Susan Huntemann, Designer; Mick Cochran, Art Director

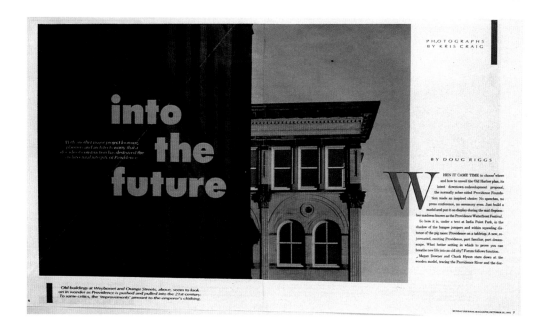

PHOTOGRAPHS BY KRIS CRAIG

into the future

BY DOUG RIGGS

WHEN IT CAME TIME to choose where and how to unveil the Old Harbor plan, its latest downtown-redevelopment proposal, the normally sober-sided Providence Foundation made an inspired choice: No speeches, no press conference, no ceremony even. Just build a model and put it on display during the mid-September madness known as the Providence Waterfront Festival. So here it is, under a tent at India Point Park, in the shadow of the bungee jumpers and within squealing distance of the pig races: Providence on a tabletop. A new, rejuvenated, exciting Providence, part familiar, part dreamscape. What better setting in which to prove you can breathe new life into an old city? Forum follows function. Megan Downer and Chuck Hyson stare down at the wooden model, tracing the Providence River and the dot-

Old buildings at Weybosset and Orange Streets, above, seem to look on in wonder as Providence is pushed and pulled into the 21st century. To some critics, the "improvements" amount to the emperor's clothing.

IMAGES FROM LAND, SEA, AND AIR CARRY US ACROSS THE YEAR.

A YEAR AGO, we seemed to be living in a state of perpetual crisis. It would be too much to say that the storm has passed, but — what a difference a year makes! Last year the scoundrels hid out or lay low; this year, they have had to face the music, and the camera. The wounds from the credit-union debacle and the recession may take many more years to heal, but it seems that, at last, the recovery has begun. In the election, voters spoke loudly in favor of ethics reform. It was a bad year for Warwick's schools, Pawtucket's water, and Queen Elizabeth — both the monarch and the ship. And except for the arrival of the Providence Bruins, it was a horrible year for local sports fans. But don't give up hope. The Jamestown-Verrazzano Bridge was completed; miracles do happen.

Sailing in for Tall Ships Newport '92 is the four-masted barkentine Esmeralda, Chile's naval-academy training ship, tallest of the vessels that took part in the July festival.
Photograph by Michael J. B. Kelly.

Captured

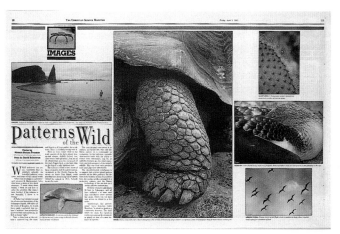

Award of Excellence

The Christian Science Monitor

Melanie Stetson Freeman, Photographer/Photo Editor

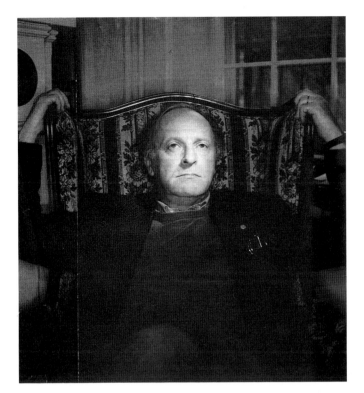

Award of Excellence

The Washington Post Magazine

Frank Olkenfels, Photographer; Richard Baker, Art Director & Designer

Award of Excellence

The Seattle Times

Harley Soltes, Photographer; Gary Settle, Photo Editor; Robin Avni, Photo Editor & Art Director, Designer; Staff Photographers

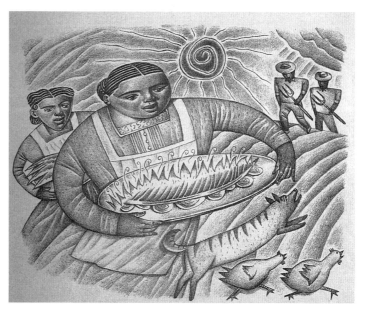

Bronze

The Des Moines Register

Mark Marturello, Artist

Silver

*The Dallas
Morning News*

Lamberto Alvarez, Illustrator
& Designer; Ed Kohorst, Art
Director

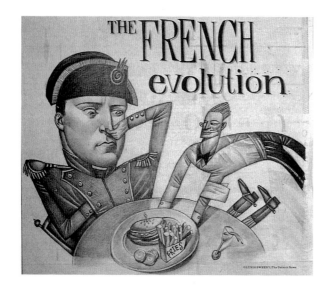

Bronze

The Detroit News

Glynis Sweeny, Illustrator & Designer; Wes Bausmith, Art Director

Bronze

The Detroit News

Glynis Sweeny, Illustrator & Designer; Wes Bausmith, Art Director

Bronze

The Miami Herald

Phill Flanders, Illustrator; Rich Bard, Viewpoint Editor; Randy Stano, Director/Editorial
Art & Design

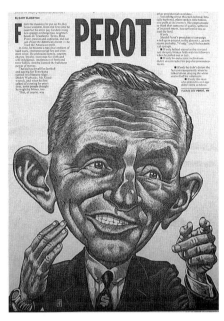

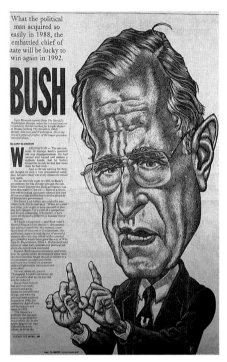

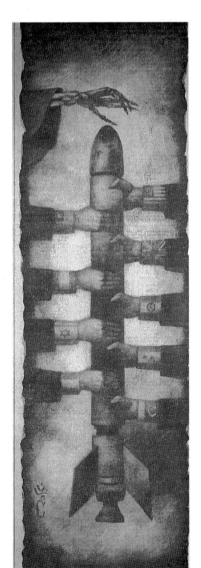

Bronze

San Jose Mercury News

Sydney Fisher, Illustrator & Designer; Bryan Monroe, Design Director; Bob
Reynolds, Art Director

Bronze

The Toronto Star

Raffi Anderian, Illustrator; Jim Harrison, Designer; Ian
Somerville, Art Director

Bronze & JSR

El Mundo

Madrid, Spain

Ricardo Martinez, Illustration Editor

Bronze & JSR

El Mundo

Madrid, Spain

Ricardo Martinez, Illustration Editor

Award of Excellence & JSR

El Mundo

Madrid, Spain

Ricardo Martinez, Illustration Editor

Award of Excellence & JSR

El Mundo

Madrid, Spain

Ricardo Martinez, Illustration Editor

Award of Excellence

Detroit Free Press

John Labbe, Illustrator; Deborah Withey, Design
Director

Award of Excellence

Detroit Free Press

Michael Prinzo, Illustrator; Andrew J. Hartley, Art
Director; Deborah Withey, Design Director

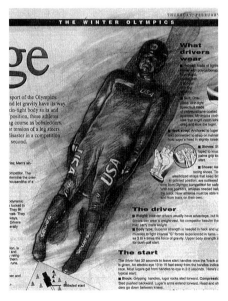

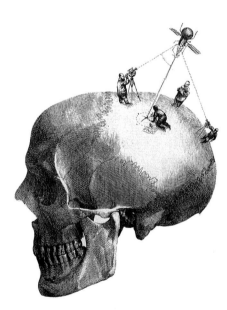

Award of Excellence

The Detroit News

Glynis Sweeny, Illustrator & Designer; Wes Bausmith,
Art Director

Award of Excellence

The Detroit News

Patrick Sedlar, Graphics Artist; Kenneth Knight,
Graphics Artist; Sidney Jablonski, Graphics Artist;
Michele Fecht, Assistant Graphics Editor & Researcher;
Robert Graham, Art Director; Brian Handley, Assistant
Sports Editor

Award of Excellence

El Mundo

Madrid, Spain

Carmelo Caderot, Art Director & Designer; Ulises
Culebro, Illustrator

Award of Excellence

The Miami Herald

Patterson Clark, Graphics Artist; Rich Bard, Viewpoint
Editor; Randy Stano, Director/Editorial Art & Design

Award of Excellence

The Lowell Sun

Lowell, MA

Andrea Wisnewski, Illustrator; Mitchell J. Hayes, Art
Director & Designer; Carol McQuaid, Editor

Award of Excellence

El Nuevo Dia

San Juan, PR

Jose L. Diaz de Villegas Sr., Art Director, Designer &
Illustrator

Award of Excellence

The Miami Herald

Patterson Clark, Graphics Artist; Rich Bard, Viewpoint
Editor; Randy Stano, Director/Editorial Art & Design

Award of Excellence

The Miami Herald

Patterson Clark, Graphics Artist; Randy Stano,
Director/Editorial Art & Design

Award of Excellence

The Detroit News

Don Asmussen, Illustrator & Designer; Felix Grabowski,
Art Director; Dierck Casselman, AME Graphics/Design

Award of Excellence
Newsday
Gary Viskupic, Illustrator

Award of Excellence
The New York Times
Steven Salerno, Illustrator; Barbara Richer, Art Director
& Designer

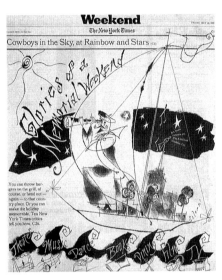

Award of Excellence
The National Law Journal
New York, NY
Christopher Bing, Illustrator; Douglas Hunt, Design
Director

Award of Excellence
The New York Times
Horacio Cardo, Illustrator; Jerelle
Kraus, Art Director & Designer

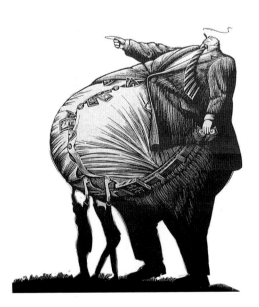

Award of Excellence
The Detroit News
Don Asmussen, Illustrator & Designer; Felix Grabowski,
Art Director

Award of Excellence
The Miami Herald
Patterson Clark, Graphics Artist; Rich Bard, Viewpoint Editor;
Randy Stano, Director/Editorial Art & Design

Award of Excellence
The Village Voice

Steve Brodner, Illustrator; Robert Newman, Design
Director; Florian Bachleda, Designer

Award of Excellence
The Wall Street Journal

Thomas Kerr, Illustrator; Greg Leeds, Designer &
Design Director

Award of Excellence
San Jose Mercury News

Molly Swisher, Illustrator & Designer; Bob Reynolds, Art
Director

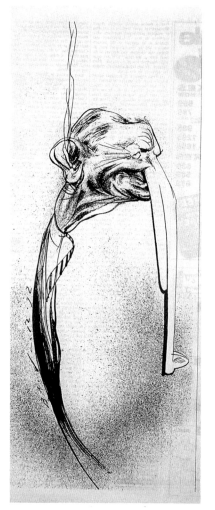

Award of Excellence
*San Francisco
Examiner*

Gordon Studer, Artist/Designer;
Kelly Frankeny, Art Director

Award of Excellence
The Toronto Star

Patrick Corrigan, Graphics Artist

Silver

The Detroit News

Glynis Sweeny, Designer; Wes Bausmith, Art Director

Silver

The Akron Beacon Journal/Beacon Magazine

Akron, OH

Tim Jonke, Illustrator; Dennis Balogh, Art Director

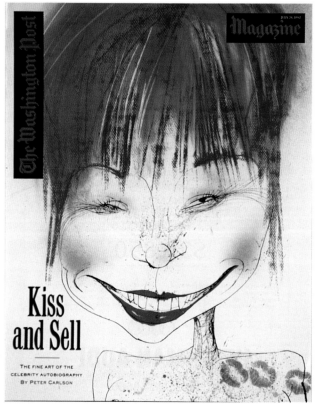

Silver

The Washington Post Magazine

David Hughes, Illustrator; Kelly Doe, Art Director & Designer

Bronze

Anchorage Daily News

Pete Spino, Designer & Illustrator

Bronze

Detroit Free Press

Rick Sealock, Illustrator; Claire Innes, Art Director

Bronze

El Nuevo Herald

Miami, FL

Nuri Ducassi, Art Director Designer & Illustrator

Bronze

Anchorage Daily News

Joel Peter Johnson, Illustrator; Galie Jean-Louis, Features Design Director; Julliete Torrez, Features Designer

Bronze
The New York Times Magazine
Owen Smith, Illustrator; Janet Froelich, Art Director; Kandy Littrell, Designer

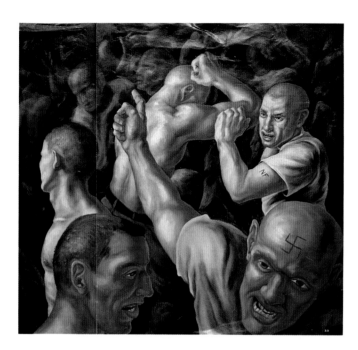

Bronze
The Washington Post Magazine
Jeanne Berg, Illustrator; Richard Baker, Art Director & Designer

Bronze
The Virginian-Pilot/Ledger-Star
Norfolk, VA
Ken Wright, Graphics Artist

Bronze
The Washington Post Magazine
Robert Goldstrom, Illustrator; Richard Baker, Art Director

Award of Excellence

Anchorage Daily News

Dee Boyles, Illustrator; Galie Jean-Louis, Features
Design Director

Award of Excellence

The Boston Globe

Joseph Daniel Fiedler, Illustrator; Lucy Bartholomay,
Art Director & Designer

Award of Excellence

The Boston Globe

Gary Baseman, Illustrator; Cynthia Hoffman, Art
Director & Designer

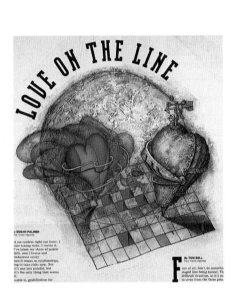

Award of Excellence

Computer Reseller News

Manhasset, NY

Tim Jessel, Illustrator; Gene Fedele, Senior Art Director;
Marc Taffet, Senior Designer; Edie Platt, Production; Liz
Gallagher, Editor

Award of Excellence

Detroit Free Press

David Myatt, Illustrator; Andrew J. Hartley, Art
Director; Deborah Withey, Design Director

Award of Excellence

Detroit Free Press

Dave Cutler, Illustrator; Andrew J. Hartley, Art Director
& Designer; Deborah Withey, Design Director

Award of Excellence
The Miami Herald

John Kascht, Illustrator; Rhonda Prast, Features Design
Editor; Herman Vega, Designer

Award of Excellence
The Miami Herald

John Kascht, Illustrator; Rhonda Prast, Features Design
Editor; Herman Vega, Designer

Award of Excellence
The Lowell Sun
Lowell, MA
Jennifer Hewittson, Illustrator; Mitchell J. Hayes, Art
Director & Designer; Carol McQuaid, Editor

Award of Excellence
The Miami Herald
Herman Vega, Illustrator

Award of Excellence
Detroit Free Press
Whitney Sherman, Illustrator; Steve Anderson, Art
Director

Award of Excellence

The Philadelphia Inquirer Magazine

Jessica Helfand, Design Director, Illustrator & Designer; Bert Fox, Art Director

Award of Excellence

The Press Democrat

Santa Rosa, CA

Sharon Henry, Illustrator & Designer

Award of Excellence

The Press Democrat

Santa Rosa, CA

Sharon Henry, Illustrator

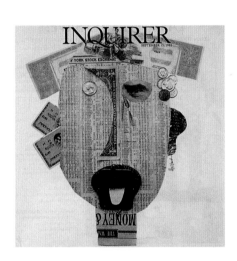

Award of Excellence

The New York Times

Etienne Delessert, Illustrator; Nancy Kent, Art Director & Designer

Award of Excellence

The Washington Post Magazine

Peter De Seve, Illustrator; Richard Baker, Art Director; Kelly Doe, Deputy Art Director, Designer; Peggy Robertson, Photographer

Award of Excellence
San Jose Mercury News

Sydney Fischer, Illustrator; Bryan Monroe, Design
Director; Molly Swisher, Art Director

Award of Excellence
San Jose Mercury News

Sam Hundley, Illustrator

Award of Excellence
The Washington Post Magazine

Elwood Smith, Illustrator; Richard Baker, Art Director &
Designer

Award of Excellence
San Jose Mercury News

Molly Swisher, Illustrator & Designer; Bob Reynolds,
Art Director

Award of Excellence
The Washington Times

Don Asmussen, Artist; John Kascht, Art Director &
Designer

Award of Excellence
The Sacramento Bee
Sacramento, CA

James Chaffee, Editorial Artist

Silver & JSR

El Mundo

Madrid, Spain

Ricardo Martinez, Illustration Editor

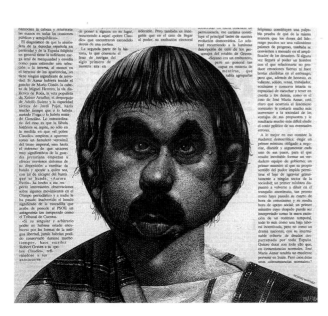

Silver

La Vanguardia

Barcelona, Spain

Perico Pastor, Illustrator; Carlos Pérez de Rozas, Art Director; Ferran Grau, Graphic Design Editor; Angels Soler, Designer; Rosa Mundet, Art Director Assistant

Bronze
The Des Moines Register
Mark Marturello, Artist

Bronze
The Christian Science Monitor
Tom Hughes, Illustrator

Bronze

The Detroit News

Glynis Sweeny, Designer/Illustrator; Wes Bausmith, Art Director

Bronze

El Nuevo Herald

Miami, FL

Nuri Ducassi, Art Director, Illustrator/Designer

Bronze

The Miami Herald

Patterson Clark, Editorial Artist; Rich Bard, Viewpoint
Editor; Randy Stano, Director/Editorial Art & Design

Award of Excellence

Computer Reseller News

Manhasset, NY

Nicholas Wilton, Illustrator; Gene Fedele, Senior Art Director; Dave Nicastro,
Production

Award of Excellence

Anchorage Daily News

Dee Boyles, Illustrator; Galie Jean-Louis, Design Director

Award of Excellence

The Akron Beacon Journal/Beacon Magazine
Akron, OH
Dennis Balogh, Illustrator & Designer

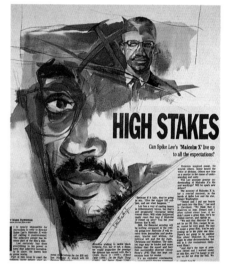

Award of Excellence

The Albuquerque Tribune

Jeff Neumann, Designer

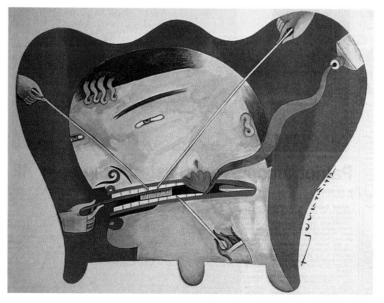

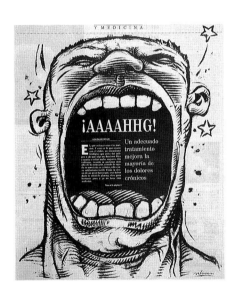

Award of Excellence

El Mundo

Madrid, Spain
Tono Benavides, Illustrator; Carmelo Caderot, Art
Director

Award of Excellence

El Mundo

Madrid, Spain
Ulises Culebro, Illustrator; Carmelo Caderot, Art
Director & Designer

Award of Excellence

El Mundo

Madrid, Spain
Samuel Velasco, Illustrator

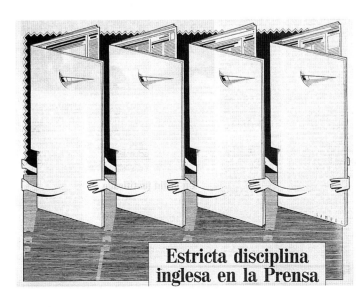

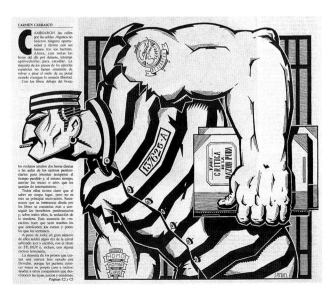

Award of Excellence

El Pais

Madrid, Spain

Loredano Casio Da Salva, Illustrator

Award of Excellence

Detroit Free Press

David Cowles, Illustrator; Steve Anderson, Art Director

Award of Excellence

El Periodico de Cataluna

Barcelona, Spain

Andrew Lucas, Designer; Jeff Goertzen, Graphics
Consultant; Xavier Conesa, Art Director

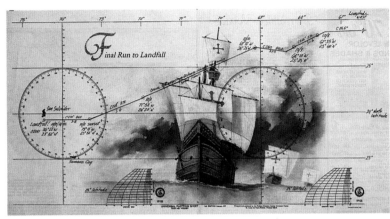

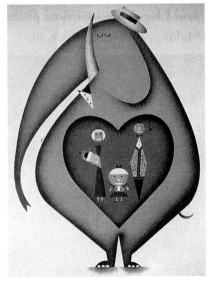

Award of Excellence
Providence Sunday Journal Magazine
Providence, RI
Frank Gerardi, Illustrator

Award of Excellence
The New York Times Magazine
Terry Allen, Illustrator; Janet Froelich, Art Director;
Daryl Palmas, Designer; Kathy Ryan, Photo Editor

Award of Excellence
The Orange County Register
Santa Ana, CA
Lisa Mertins, Graphics Artist

Silver

El Mundo

Madrid, Spain

Gorka Sampedro, Graphics Artist; Samuel Velasco, Graphics Artist; Dina Sanchez, Graphics Artist; Mario Tascon, Infographics Editor

Bronze

El Periodico de Cataluna

Barcelona, Spain

Jaime Serra, Designer; Jordi Catala, Designer; Ricard Gracia, Designer; Jeff Goertzen, Graphics Consultant; Xavier Conesa, Art Director

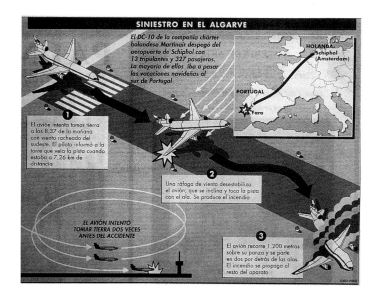

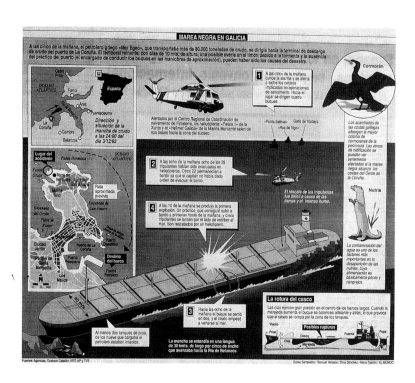

Bronze

La Vanguardia

Barcelona, Spain

Jordi Paris, Infographic Artist; Antoni Pique, Researcher; Carlos Perez de Rozas, Art Director; Rosa Mundet, Assistant Art Director

Bronze

La Vanguardia

Barcelona, Spain

Jordi Paris, Infographic Artist; Rosa M. Anechina, Infographic Artist; Antoni Pique, Researcher; Carlos Perez de Rozas, Art Director; Rosa Mundet, Assistant Art Director

Award of Excellence
The Dallas Morning News

Laura Stanton, Graphics Artist;
Lon Tweeton, Graphics Artist;
Marco Ruiz, Graphics Reporter
& Artist; Ben McConnell,
Graphics Editor; Ed Kohorst,
Art Director; Kathleen
Vincent, Deputy Art Director

Bronze
Los Angeles Times
(Orange County Edition)
Costa Mesa, CA
David Puckett, Illustrator; Lily Dow Kuroda, Graphics Editor

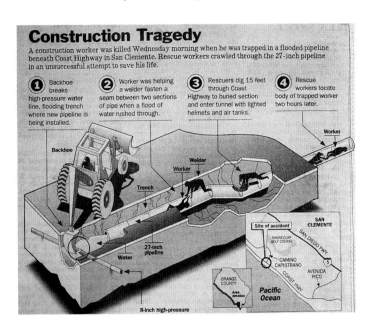

Construction Tragedy
A construction worker was killed Wednesday morning when he was trapped in a flooded pipeline beneath Coast Highway in San Clemente. Rescue workers crawled through the 27-inch pipeline in an unsuccessful attempt to save his life.

Award of Excellence
The Dallas Morning News

Marco Ruiz, Graphics Artist;
Lon Tweeton, Graphics
Artist; Ben McConnell,
Graphics Editor; Kathleen
Vincent, Deputy Art Director;
Ed Kohorst, Art Director

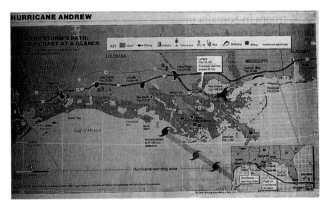

HURRICANE ANDREW

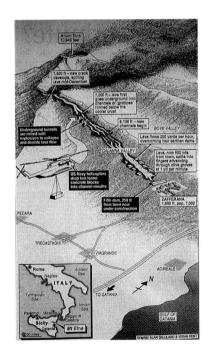

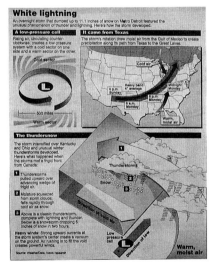

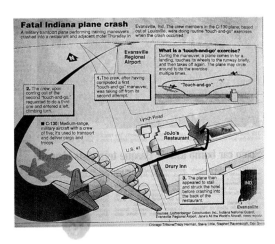

Award of Excellence
Chicago Tribune

Stephen Ravenscraft, Graphics Artist; Steve Little, Graphics Artist;
Tracy Herman, Graphics Coordinator; Don Sena, Graphics
Coordinator; Stephen Cvengros, Illustrations Editor

Award of Excellence
The Detroit News

Sidney Jablonski, Graphics Artist; Hugh McCann,
Researcher; David Pierce, Graphics Editor; Dierck
Casselman, AME Graphics/Design

Award of Excellence
The Daily Telegraph
London, England
Vivian Kent, Graphics Artist; Alan Gilliland,
Graphics Editor

Award of Excellence
El Pais
Madrid, Spain

Carmen Trejo, Graphic Journalist;
Javier Sicilia, Graphic Journalist

Award of Excellence
El Pais
Madrid, Spain

Gustavo Hermoso, Graphic Journalist

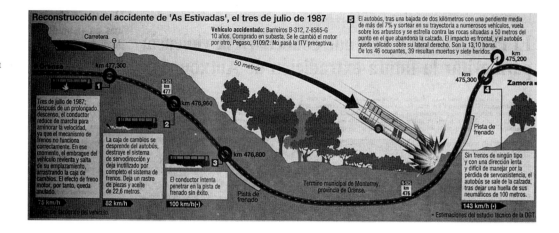

Award of Excellence
Marca
Madrid, Spain

Jose Juan Gamez, Illustrator & Designer; Pablo Ma Ramirez,
Illustrator & Designer; Martina Gil, Illustrator & Designer;
Sofia Valganon, Illustrator & Designer

Award of Excellence
Newsday

Philip Dionisio, Illustrator & Graphics Supervisor; Tim
Drachlis, Graphics Editor

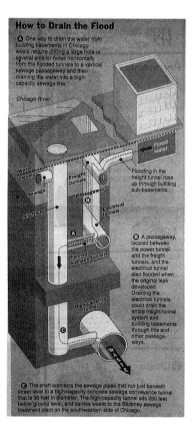

Award of Excellence
The New York Times

John Papasian, Illustrator; Ty Ahmad-Taylor,
Graphics

Award of Excellence
The Sunday Times
London, England
Gary Cook, Artist, Designer & Deputy
Graphics Editor

Award of Excellence
Richmond Times-Dispatch
Richmond, VA
Tom Roberts, Graphics Artist; Stephen Rountree, Graphics Artist

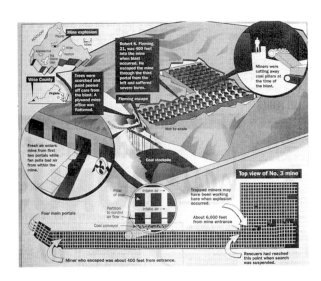

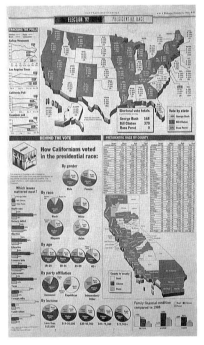

Award of Excellence
San Francisco Examiner
Chris Morris, Artist; Kelly Frankeny, Art Director

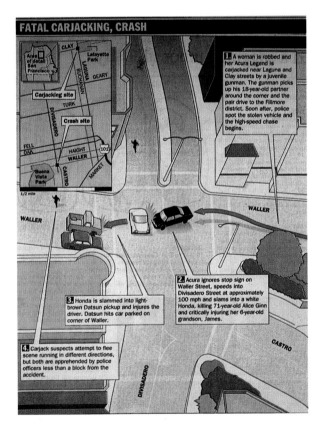

Bronze
San Francisco Examiner
Chris Morris, Artist; Kelly Frankeny, Art Director; Paul Avery, Reporter

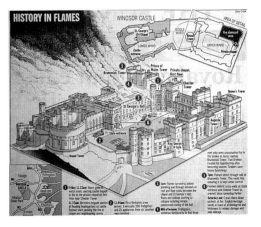

Award of Excellence
The Sunday Times
London, England
Gary Cook, Artist, Designer & Deputy Graphics Editor

Bronze
Los Angeles Times
(Orange County Edition)
Costa Mesa, CA

Scott Brown, Illustrator; Dennis Lowe, Illustrator; Danny Sullivan, Researcher; Kristina Lindgren, Researcher; Juan Thomassie, Art Director; Lily Dow Kuroda, Graphics Editor

Award of Excellence
The Times-Picayune
New Orleans, LA

James Zisk, Infographic Artist

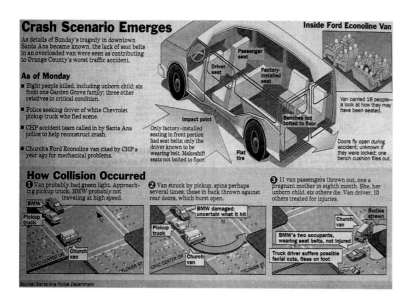

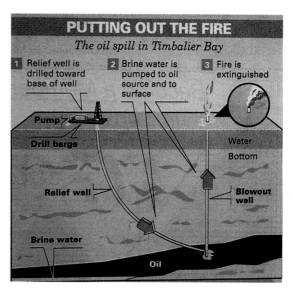

Award of Excellence
Detroit Free Press

Jonathan Massie, Artist; Laura Varon Brown, Graphics Director; Ted Williamson, Assistant Graphics Editor; Jim Schaefer, Reporter; Roger Chesley, Reporter

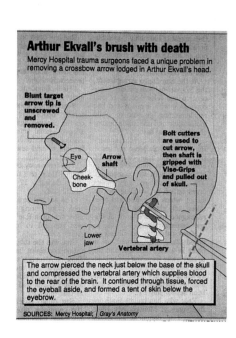

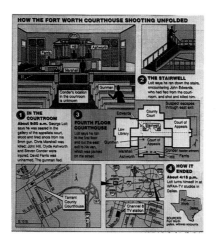

Award of Excellence
The Oregonian
Portland, OR

Michael Mode, Graphics Artist; Michelle Wise, Art Director

Award of Excellence
The San Diego Union-Tribune
San Diego, CA

Ken Marshall, Artist

Award of Excellence
The Dallas Morning News

Karen Davis, Graphics Artist; Hiram Henriquez, Graphics Artist; Ed Kohorst, News Art Director; Kathleen Shannon Vincent, Deputy News Art Director

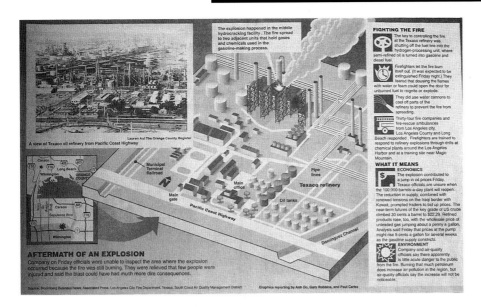

A view of Texaco oil refinery from Pacific Coast Highway

The explosion happened in the middle hydrocracking facility. The fire spread to two adjacent units that hold gases and chemicals used in the gasoline-making process.

FIGHTING THE FIRE
The key to controlling the fire at the Texaco refinery was shutting off the fuel line into the hydrogen-processing unit, where semi-refined oil is turned into gasoline and diesel fuel.

Firefighters let the fire burn itself out. (It was expected to be extinguished Friday night.) They feared that dousing the flames with water or foam could open the door for unburned fuel to reignite or explode.

They did use water cannons to cool off parts of the refinery to prevent the fire from spreading.

Thirty-four fire companies and fire-rescue ambulances from Los Angeles city. Los Angeles County and Long Beach responded. Firefighters are trained to respond to refinery explosions through drills at chemical plants around the Los Angeles Harbor and at a training site near Magic Mountain.

WHAT IT MEANS
ECONOMICS
The explosion contributed to a jump in oil prices Friday. Texaco officials are unsure when the 100,000-barrels-a-day plant will reopen. The reduction in supply, combined with renewed tensions on the Iraqi border with Kuwait, prompted traders to bid up prices. The near-term futures of the key grade of US crude climbed 30 cents a barrel to $22.29. Refined products rose, too, with the wholesale price of unleaded gas jumping about a penny a gallon. Analysts said Friday that prices at the pump might rise 5 cents a gallon for several weeks as the gasoline supply constricts.

ENVIRONMENT
Company and air-quality officials say there apparently is little acute danger to the public from the fire. Burning that much petroleum does increase air pollution in the region, but air-quality officials say the increase will not be noticeable.

AFTERMATH OF AN EXPLOSION
Company on Friday officials were unable to inspect the area where the explosion occurred because the fire was still burning. They were relieved that few people were injured and said the blast could have had much more dire consequences.

Sources: Bloomberg Business News; Associated Press; Los Angeles City Fire Department; Texaco; South Coast Air Quality Management District   Graphics reporting by Anh Do, Gary Robbins, and Paul Carbo

Silver

The Orange County Register

Santa Ana, CA

Paul Carbo, Graphics Artist; Anh Do, Reporter; Gary Robbins, Reporter

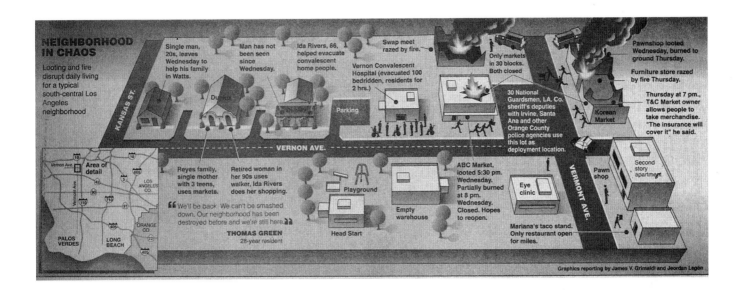

NEIGHBORHOOD IN CHAOS

Looting and fire disrupt daily living for a typical south-central Los Angeles neighborhood

Single man, 20s, leaves Wednesday to help his family in Watts.

Man has not been seen since Wednesday.

Ida Rivers, 66, helped evacuate convalescent home people.

Swap meet razed by fire.

Vernon Convalescent Hospital (evacuated 100 bedridden, residents for 2 hrs.)

Only markets in 30 blocks. Both closed

Pawnshop looted Wednesday, burned to ground Thursday.

Furniture store razed by fire Thursday.

Thursday at 7 pm., T&C Market owner allows people to take merchandise. "The insurance will cover it" he said.

30 National Guardsmen, L.A. Co. sheriff's deputies with Irvine, Santa Ana and other Orange County police agencies use this lot as deployment location.

Korean Market

Area of detail

Reyes family, single mother with 3 teens, uses markets.

Retired woman in her 90s uses walker, Ida Rivers does her shopping.

ABC Market, looted 5:30 pm. Wednesday. Partially burned at 8 pm. Wednesday. Closed. Hopes to reopen.

Eye clinic

Pawn shop

Second story apartment

"We'll be back. We can't be smashed down. Our neighborhood has been destroyed before and we're still here."
THOMAS GREEN
28-year resident

Playground

Head Start

Empty warehouse

Mariana's taco stand. Only restaurant open for miles.

Graphics reporting by James V. Grimaldi and Jeordan Legón

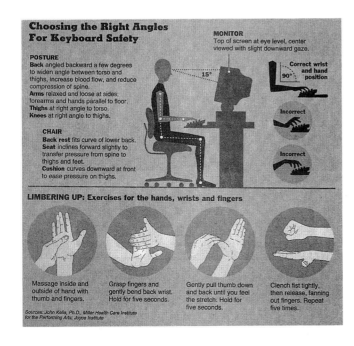

Choosing the Right Angles For Keyboard Safety

POSTURE
Back angled backward a few degrees to widen angle between torso and thighs, increase blood flow, and reduce compression of spine.
Arms relaxed and loose at sides; forearms and hands parallel to floor.
Thighs at right angle to torso.
Knees at right angle to thighs.

CHAIR
Back rest fits curve of lower back.
Seat inclines forward slightly to transfer pressure from spine to thighs and feet.
Cushion curves downward at front to ease pressure on thighs.

MONITOR
Top of screen at eye level, center viewed with slight downward gaze.

15°

Correct wrist and hand position
90°

Incorrect

Incorrect

LIMBERING UP: Exercises for the hands, wrists and fingers

Massage inside and outside of hand with thumb and fingers.

Grasp fingers and gently bend back wrist. Hold for five seconds.

Gently pull thumb down and back until you feel the stretch. Hold for five seconds.

Clench fist tightly, then release, fanning out fingers. Repeat five times.

Sources: John Kella, Ph.D., Miller Health Care Institute for the Performing Arts; Joyce Institute

Silver

The New York Times

Megan Jaegerman, Researcher, Designer & Illustrator

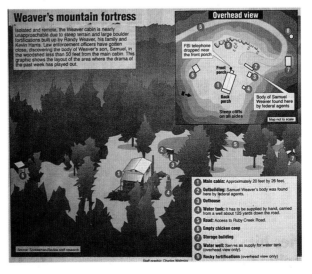

Weaver's mountain fortress

Isolated and remote, the Weaver cabin is nearly unapproachable due to steep terrain and large boulder fortifications built up by Randy Weaver, his family and Kevin Harris. Law enforcement officers have gotten close, discovering the body of Weaver's son, Samuel, in the woodshed less than 50 feet from the main cabin. This graphic shows the layout of the area where the drama of the past week has played out.

Overhead view

FBI telephone dropped near the front porch

Front porch

Back porch

Body of Samuel Weaver found here by federal agents

Steep cliffs on all sides

Map not to scale

1. **Main cabin:** Approximately 20 feet by 26 feet.
2. **Outbuilding:** Samuel Weaver's body was found here by federal agents.
3. **Outhouse**
4. **Water tank:** It has to be supplied by hand, carried from a well about 125 yards down the road.
5. **Road:** Access to Ruby Creek Road.
6. **Empty chicken coop**
7. **Storage building**
8. **Water well:** Serves as supply for water tank (overhead view only).
9. **Rocky fortifications** (overhead view only)

Source: Spokesman-Review staff research

Staff graphic: Charles Waltmire

Award of Excellence

The Spokesman-Review

Spokane, WA

Charles Waltmire, Graphics Artist; Vince Grippi, Graphics Editor

Silver
The New York Times

Megan Jaegerman, Researcher, Designer & Illustrator

Silver
Newsday

Steve Madden, Graphics Artist; Tim Drachlis, Graphics

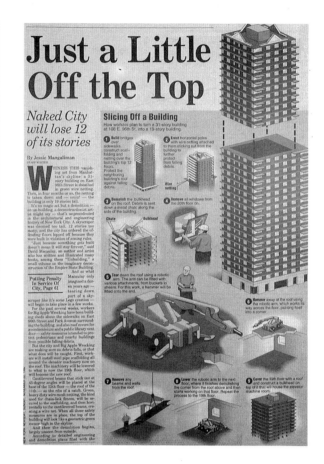

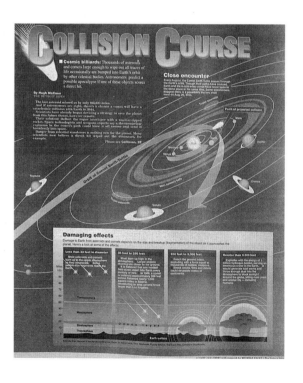

Bronze
The Baltimore Sun

Joseph Hutchinson, Graphics Director

Bronze
The Detroit News

Sidney Jablonski, Artist & Designer; Michele Fecht, Assistant Graphics
Editor & Researcher; Robert Graham, Art Director

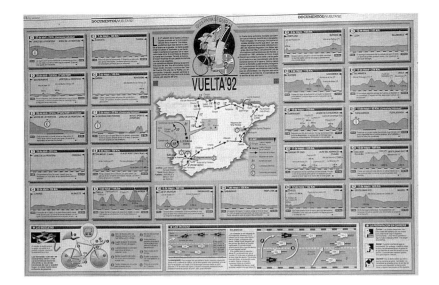

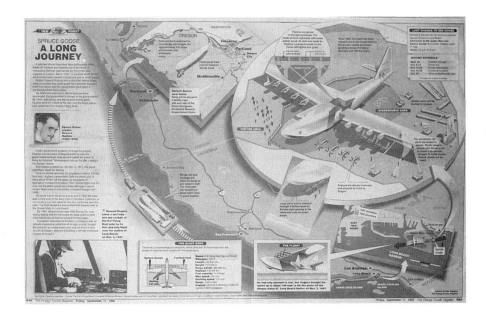

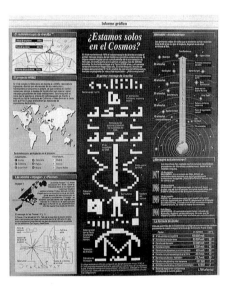

Bronze
El Mundo
Madrid, Spain

Juan Velasco, Graphics Artist; Javier Munoz, Graphics Artist; Modesto J. Carrasco, Graphics Artist Editor

Award of Excellence
Akron Beacon Journal
Akron, OH

Terence Oliver, Artist; John Backderf, Artist; Brian Shelito, Artist

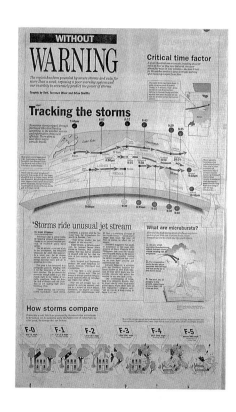

Award of Excellence
El Pais
Madrid, Spain

Jordi Clapers, Graphic Journalist

Award of Excellence
The Detroit News

J. Patrick Sedlar, Artist & Designer; Scott Faust, Assistant City Editor; Michele Fecht, Assistant Graphics Editor

Award of Excellence
Detroit Free Press

Jonathan Massie, Graphics Artist; Ted Williamson, Assistant Graphics Editor; Julian Gonzalez, Photographer; Laura Varon Brown, Graphics Director

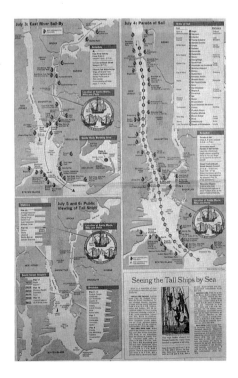

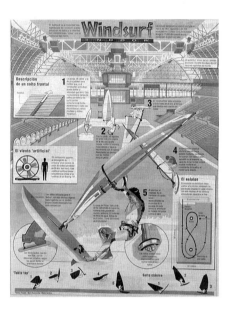

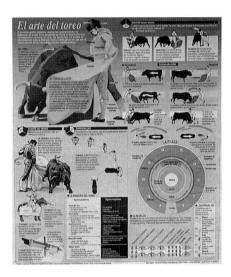

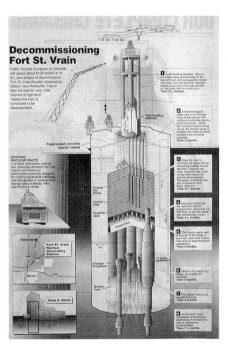

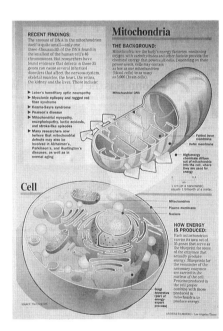

Award of Excellence

The New York Times

Natasha Perkel, Artist; John Papasian, Artist; Steve
Hadermayer, Artist; Genevieve Williams, Art Director

Award of Excellence

Rocky Mountain News

Denver, CO

Tim Williams, Chief Artist

Award of Excellence

Los Angeles Times

Anders Ramberg, Illustrator & Designer; Sara Lessley,
Graphics Coordinator

Gold

AP/El Mundo/El Periodico de Cataluna

Madrid, Spain

Andrew Lucas, Illustrator; Karl Gude, Infographic Editor; Mario Tascon, Infographic Editor; Xavier Conesa, Infographic Editor; Roberto Dominguez, Infographic Editor; Jeff Goertzen, Art Director; *El Mundo* Staff; El Periodico Staff; Associated Press Staff

Award of Excellence

Rocky Mountain News

Denver, CO

Eric Baker, Graphics Artist

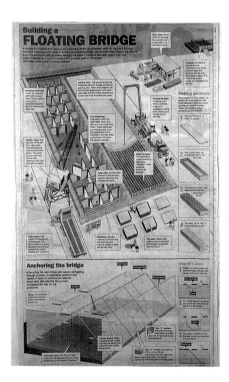

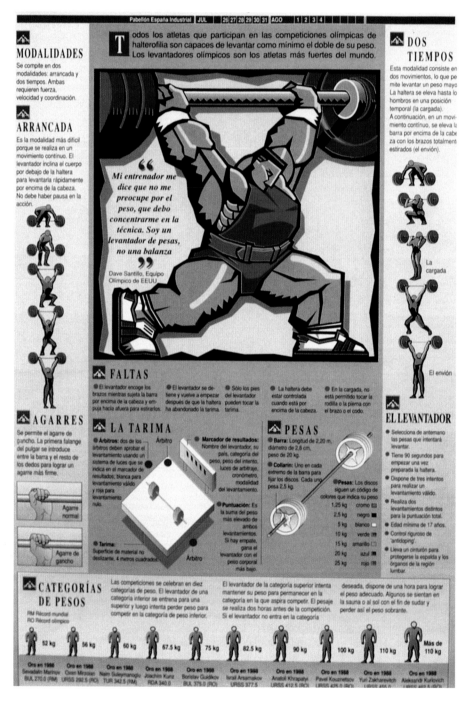

Award of Excellence

Seattle Post-Intelligencer

Seattle, WA

David Gray, Art Director, Researcher & Artist

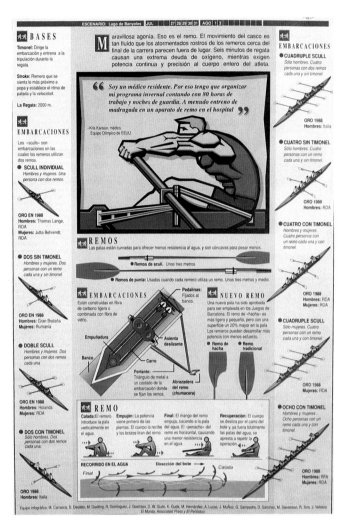

Silver
AP/El Mundo/El Periodico de Cataluna

Madrid, Spain

Silver
AP/El Mundo/El Periodico de Cataluna

Madrid, Spain

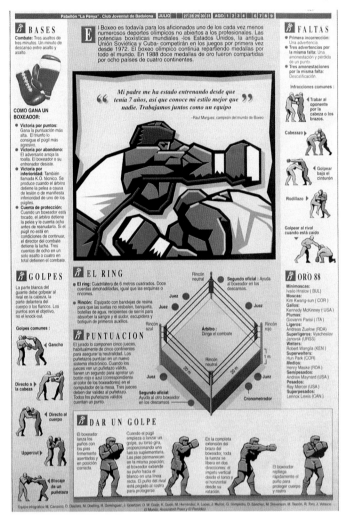

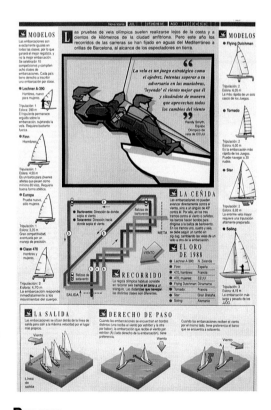

Silver

El Pais

Madrid, Spain

Staff

Bronze
AP/El Mundo/El Periodico de Cataluna

Madrid, Spain

Silver

The Orange County Register

Santa Ana, CA

Paul Carbo, Graphics Artist; Ron Campbell, Reporter; Venetia Lai, News Editor/Visuals (Graphics)

Silver

The Oregonian

Portland, OR

Steve Cowden, Illustrator; Michelle Wise, Art Director; Rick Bella, Writer

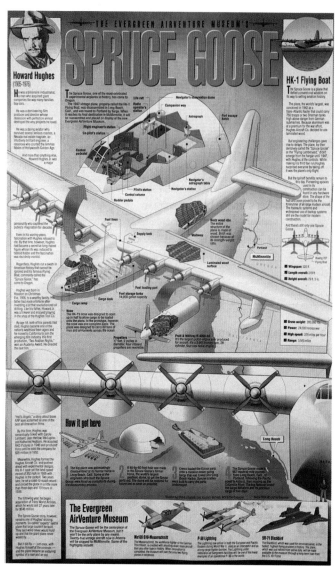

Bronze

The Daily News

Dartmouth, NS, Canada

Jamie Hutt, Design Editor

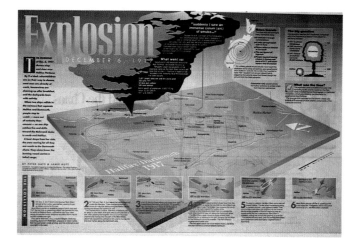

Bronze

El Periodico de Cataluna

Barcelona, Spain

Jeff Goertzen, Designer & Graphics Consultant; Jaime Serra, Designer; Andrew Lucas, Designer; Xavier Conesa, Art Director

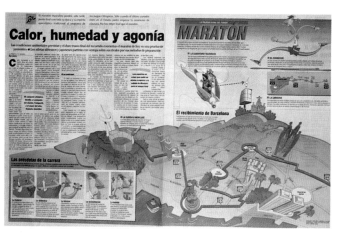

Bronze

The Hartford Courant

Hartford, CT

Patricia Cousins, Illustrator; Merle Nacht, Illustrator; Patti Nelson, Designer; Beth Messina, Designer

Bronze

Los Angeles Times

(Orange County Edition)
Costa Mesa, CA

Scott M. Brown, Illustrator; Danny Sullivan, Researcher; Juan Thomassie, Art Director; Tom Reinken, Deputy Graphics Editor

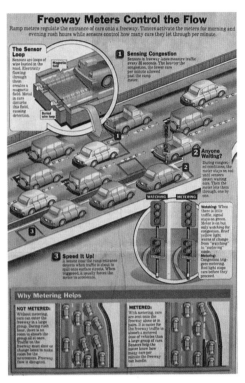

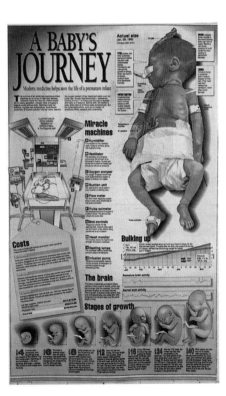

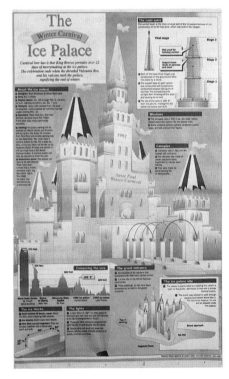

Bronze

The Virginian-Pilot/Ledger-Star

Norfolk, VA

Bill Pitzer, Illustrator & Designer

Bronze

The Oregonian

Portland, OR

Steve Cowden, Illustrator; Mark Wigginton, Art Director; Patrick O'Neill, Writer

Bronze

Saint Paul Pioneer Press

St. Paul, MN

Alex Leary, Graphics Artist; Richard Sanchez, Graphics Artist; Nancy Ward, Graphics Coordinator/Designer; Stacy Sweat, Art Director; Lucy Dalglish, Assistant News Editor

Bronze

El Periodico de Cataluna

Barcelona, Spain

Andrew Lucas, Designer;
Francina Cortes, Designer; Jeff
Goertzen, Graphics Consultant;
Xavier Conesa, Art Director

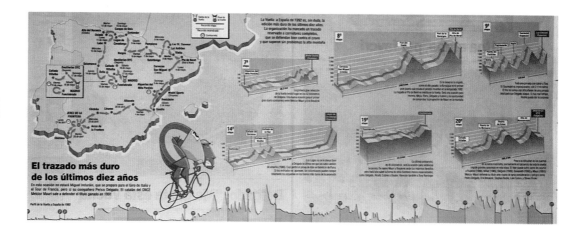

Award of Excellence

The Virginian-Pilot/Ledger-Star

Norfolk, VA

Bill Pitzer, Illustrator, Designer & Writer

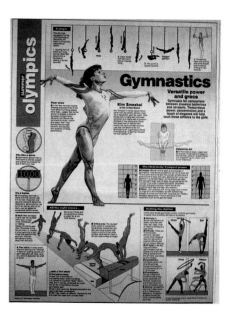

Award of Excellence

Asbury Park Press

Neptune, NJ

George Frederick, Artist & Designer; Tom Kerr,
Illustrator; Andrew Prendimano, Art Director

Award of Excellence

El Mundo Deportivo

Barcelona, Spain

Jose Antonio Alvarez, Illustrator

Award of Excellence

Chicago Tribune

Stephen Ravenscraft, Graphics Artist; Omer D. Vasin,
Graphics Artist; Scott Holingue, Graphics Artist; Rick
Tuma, Graphics Artist; Steve Little, Graphics Artist; Don
Sena, Graphics Coordinator; Tracy Herman, Graphics
Coordinator; Nancy I.Z. Reese, Graphics Coordinator;
Julie Sheer, Graphics Coordinator; Dennis Odom,
Assistant Art Director; Stephen Cvengros, Illustrations
Editor

Award of Excellence
Anchorage Daily News

Lance Lekander, Illustrator; David Hulen, Researcher; Mike Campbell, Designer & AME/Graphics; Bob Hallinen, Photographer; Dave Jones, Copy Editor

Award of Excellence
Detroit Free Press

Martha Thierry, Graphics Artist; John Green, Graphics Artist; Laura Varon Brown, Graphics Director; A.J. Hartley, Designer

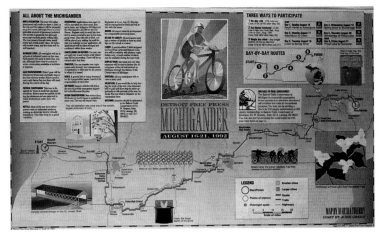

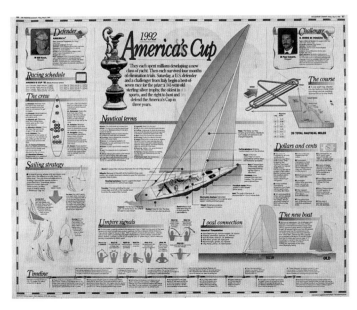

Award of Excellence
Seattle Post-Intelligencer
Ben Garrison, Graphics Artist

Award of Excellence
The Detroit News
Sidney Jablonski, Graphics Artist; Michele Fecht, Assistant Graphics Editor; Felix Grabowski, Graphics Director

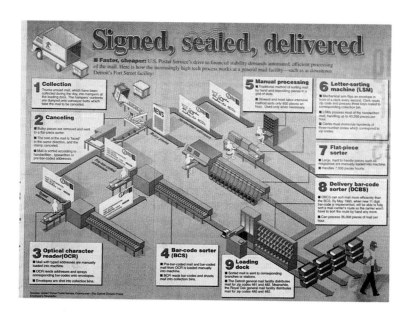

Award of Excellence
Los Angeles Times
Juan Thomassie, Graphics Artist; Vicky McCargar, Associate Graphics Editor; Sara Lessley, Graphics Coordinator

Award of Excellence
Los Angeles Times
(Orange County Edition)
Costa Mesa, CA
Dennis Lowe, Illustrator; Russ Arasmith, Illustrator; Danny Sullivan, Researcher; Marla Cone, Researcher; Tom Reinken, Deputy Graphics Editor; Lily Dow Kuroda, Graphics Editor

Award of Excellence
Los Angeles Times
Patricia Mitchell, Artist & Art Director; Victoria McCargar, Graphics Editor & Researcher; Sara Lessley, Graphics Coordinator; Helene Webb, Researcher

Award of Excellence
San Jose Mercury News
Molly Swisher, Illustrator & Designer; Bob Reynolds, Art Director

Award of Excellence
The Oregonian
Portland, OR
Michael Mode, Graphics Artist; Michelle Wise, Art Director

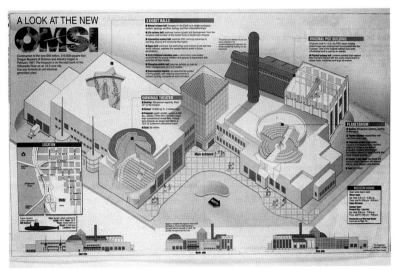

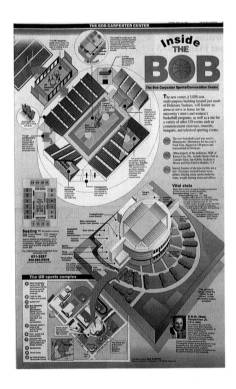

Award of Excellence
The News Journal
Wilmington, DE
Dan Garrow, Graphics Artist

Award of Excellence
The Miami Herald
Woody Vondracek, Editorial Artist; Fred Tasker, Staff
Writer; Rhonda Prast, Features Design Editor; Randy
Stano, Director/Editorial Art & Design

Award of Excellence
The Miami Herald
Woody Vondracek, Graphics Artist; Rhonda Prast,
Features Editor; Herman Vega, Designer; Randy Stano,
Director/Editorial Art & Design

Award of Excellence

San Francisco Examiner

Chris Morris, Artist; Joe Shoulak, Artist; Kelly Frankeny, Art
Director; Metro Staff, Research/Reporting

Award of Excellence

Svenska Dagbladet

Stockholm, Sweden

Bengt Salomonson, Artist & Art Director

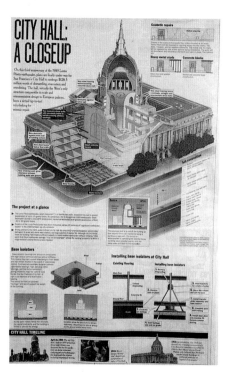

Award of Excellence

Reno Gazette-Journal

Reno, NV

David Hardman, Graphics Director; Ward Bushee,
Executive Editor; Tonia Cunning, ME

Award of Excellence

San Francisco Examiner

Chris Morris, Artist; Kelly Frankeny, Art Director;
Stewart Huntington, Research; Gerry Adams, Research

Award of Excellence

Saint Paul Pioneer Press

St. Paul, MN

Alex Leary, Graphics Artist; Nancy Ward, Graphics
Coordinator

The Sunday Times

London, England

Gary Cook, Graphics Artist; Chris Sargent, Graphics Artist; Ian Moores, Graphics Artist; Ian Bott, Graphics Artist; Phil Green, Graphics Editor

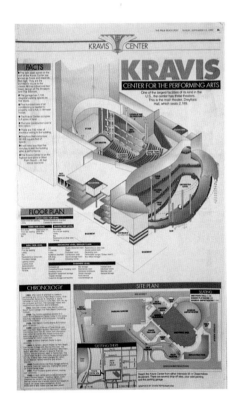

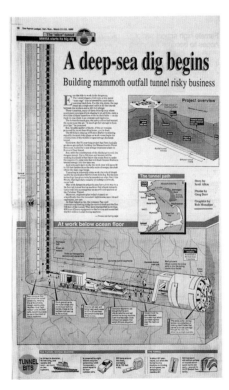

Award of Excellence

The Palm Beach Post

W. Palm Beach, FL

Vivian Rippe, Graphics Artist; Lisa M. Griffis, Art Director

Award of Excellence

The Patriot Ledger

Quincy, MA

Bob Monahan, Graphics Artist

Award of Excellence

Syracuse Herald American

Syracuse, NY

Darren A. Sanefski, Graphics Artist; Geoff Stickel, Art Director

Gold

AP/El Mundo/El Periodico de Cataluna

Madrid, Spain

Andrew Lucas, Illustrator; Karl Gude, Infographic Editor; Mario Tascon, Infographic Editor; Xavier Conesa, Infographic Editor; Roberto Dominguez, Infographic Editor; Jeff Goertzen, Art Director; *El Mundo* Staff; El Periodico Staff; Associated Press Staff

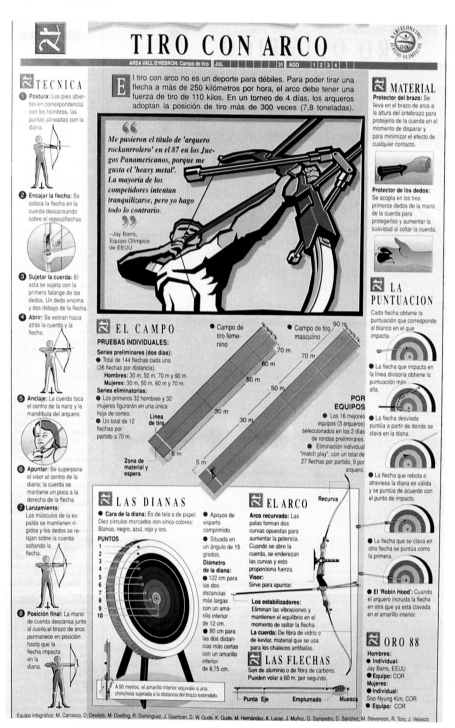

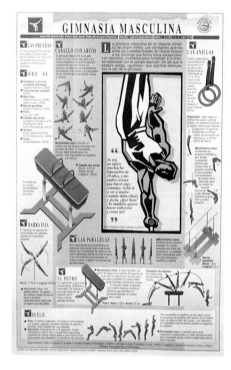

Silver

The Oregonian

Portland, OR

Steve Cowden, Illustrator; Mark Wigginton, Art Director

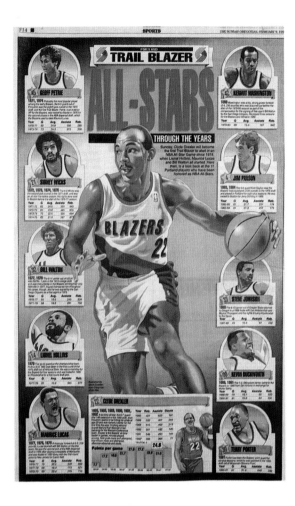

Silver

El Mundo

Madrid, Spain

Juan Velasco, Graphics Artist

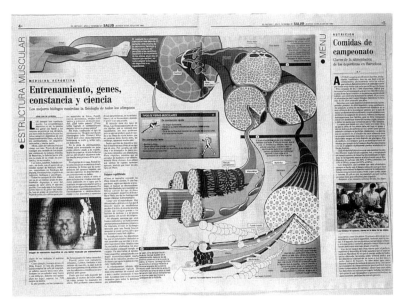

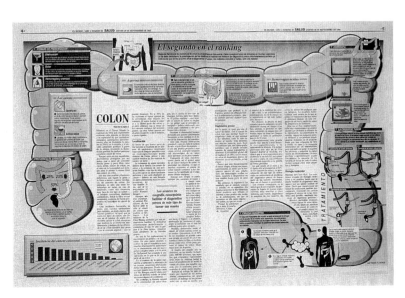

Bronze

The New York Times

Megan Jaegerman, Researcher, Designer & Illustrator;
Margaret O'Connor, Art Director; Rich Meislin, Graphics
Editor

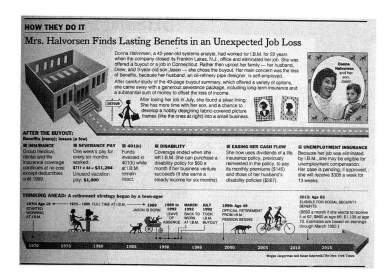

HOW THEY DO IT

Mrs. Halvorsen Finds Lasting Benefits in an Unexpected Job Loss

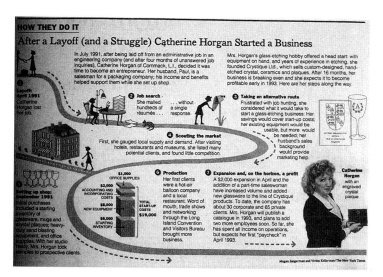

HOW THEY DO IT

After a Layoff (and a Struggle) Catherine Horgan Started a Business

Bronze

Los Angeles Times

(Orange County Edition)
Costa Mesa, CA

David Puckett, Illustrator; Juan Thomassie, Art Director; Tom Reinken,
Deputy Graphics Editor; Danny Sullivan, Researcher; Marla Cone, Researcher

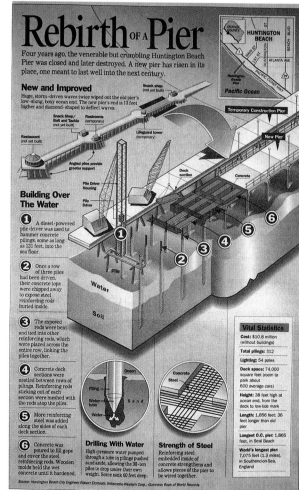

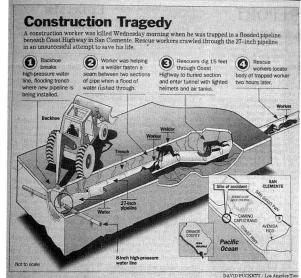

Bronze

The Orange County Register

Santa Ana, CA

Paul Carbo, Graphics Artist; Kate Cohen, Reporter; Venetia Lai, News Editor/Visuals (Graphics)

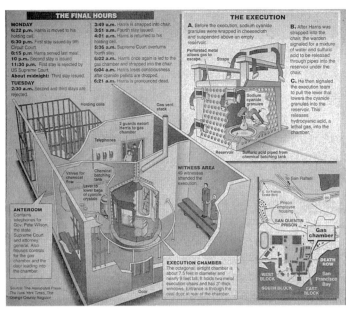

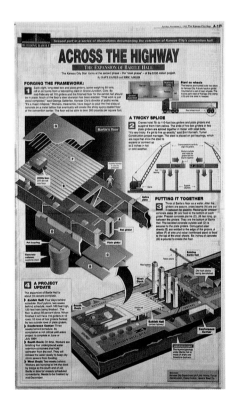

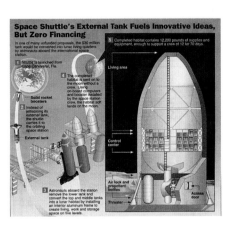

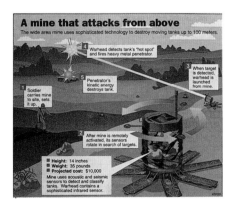

Award of Excellence

Army Times Publishing Company

Springfield, VA

Joanne Ostendorf, Graphics Artist

Award of Excellence

The Kansas City Star

Dave Eames, Graphics Artist

Award of Excellence
The Detroit News

Patrick Sedlar, Artist & Designer; Robert
Graham, Art Director; Felix Grabowski,
Graphics Director; Dierck Casselman,
AME Graphics/Design

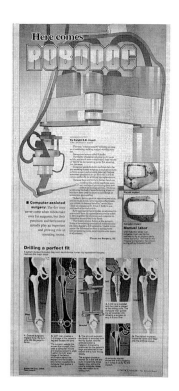

Award of Excellence
La Vanguardia

Barcelona, Spain

Arantza Alza, Graphics Artist; Josep Lluis Boveda,
Researcher; Carlos Perez de Rozas, Art Director; Rosa
Mundet, Assistant Art Director

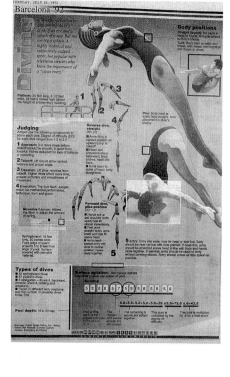

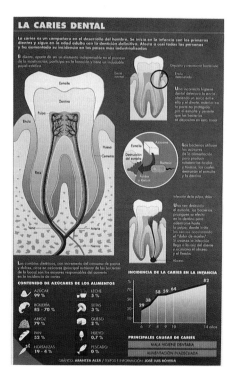

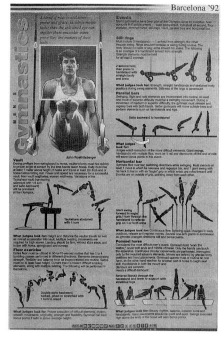

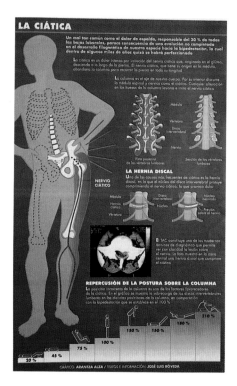

Award of Excellence
The Detroit News

Patrick Sedlar, Graphics Artist; Robert Graham, Art
Director & Designer; Felix Grabowski, Graphics
Coordinator; Dierck Casselman, AME Graphics/Design

Award of Excellence

The Virginian-Pilot/Ledger-Star

Norfolk, VA

Bill Pitzer, Illustrator & Designer

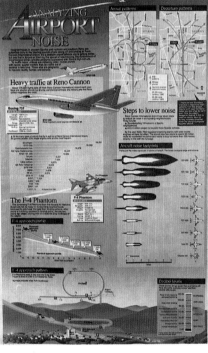

Award of Excellence

Reno Gazette-Journal

Reno, NV

Paul Horn, Graphics Artist; David Hardman, Graphics Director; Ward Bushee, Executive Editor; Tonia Cunning, ME

Award of Excellence

El Mundo

Madrid, Spain

Modesto Carrasco, Graphics Artist; Gorka Sampedro, Graphics Artist; Ramon Ramos, Graphics Artist; Dina Sanchez, Graphics Artist; Jaime de Andres, Graphics Artist; Samuel Velasco, Graphics Artist; Elena Labrado, Graphics Artist; Mario Tascon, Graphics Editor

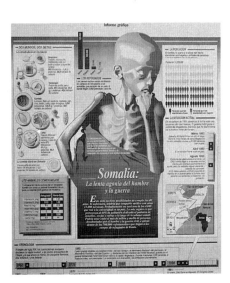

Award of Excellence

Los Angeles Times

Anders Ramberg, Designer; Jim Schachter, Assistant Business Editor; Pat Konley, Assistant News Editor

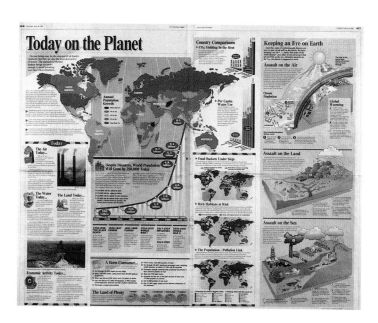

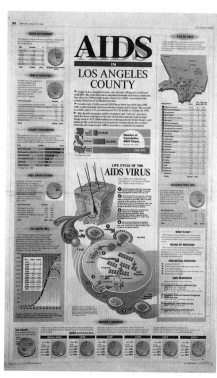

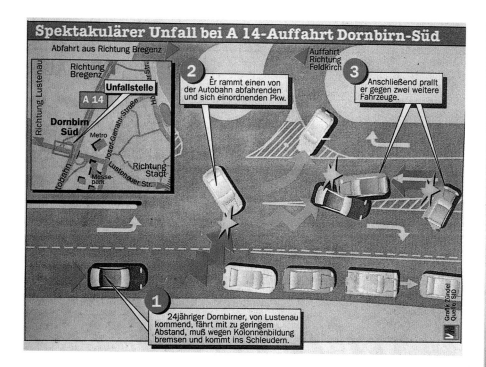

Award of Excellence

Vorarlberger Nachrichten

Bregenz, Austria

Rudolf Zundel, Art Director

Award of Excellence

The Orange County Register

Santa Ana, CA

George Turney, Graphics Artist

The Christian Science Monitor

Shirley Horn, Graphics Artist

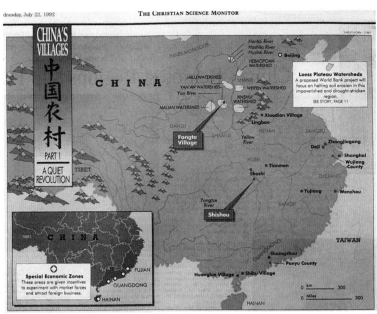

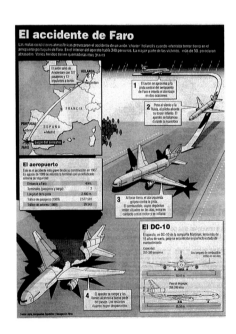

El Periodico de Cataluna

Barcelona, Spain

Jaime Serra, Designer; Jeff Goertzen, Graphics Consultant; Xavier
Conesa, Art Director

Bronze
The San Diego Union-Tribune
Randy Wright, AME Graphics; Bill Gaspard, Graphics Director; Staff

BEFORE

Award of Excellence
The Bellingham Herald
Cincinnati, OH

Ron Huff, Consultant; Jim Dean, Consultant; Staff

BEFORE

Award of Excellence
Diario de Noticias
Lisboa, Portugal

Mario Bettencourt Resendes, Editor in Chief; Joao Fragoso Mendes, Deputy Editor in Chief; Luis Delgado, Deputy Editor in Chief; Jose Maria Ribeirinho, Art Director; Jose Silva Pires, Supplements Editor; Maria Jose Lima, Deputy Art Director; Rui Coutinho, Photo Editor; Mario Garcia, Designer; Jeff Goertzen, Infographics Consultant

BEFORE

AFTER

AFTER

AFTER

MISCELLANEOUS / Overall Redesign

Award of Excellence

La Republica

San Jose, Costa Rica

Eduardo Danilo Ruiz, Design Consultant

BEFORE

Award of Excellence

The Oregonian

Portland, OR

Tim Harrower, Designer; Mark Wigginton, Art Director

BEFORE

Award of Excellence

San Jose Mercury News

Bryan Monroe, Design Director; David Yarnold, Deputy
Managing Editor; Jeff Thomas, Executive News Editor;
Sue Morrow, Picture Editor; Bob Reynolds, Art Director;
Molly Swisher, Art Director; Sam Hundley, Features
Design Director; Mike Jenner, Consultant; David Griffin,
Consultant; Bill Marr, Consultant

BEFORE

AFTER

AFTER

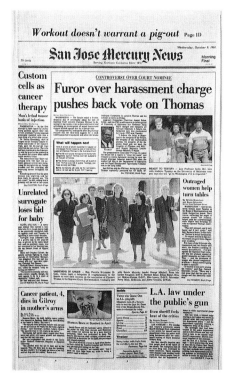

AFTER

Silver

The Wall Street Journal Reports

Louis Fischauf, Designer; Greg Leeds, Designer & Design Director

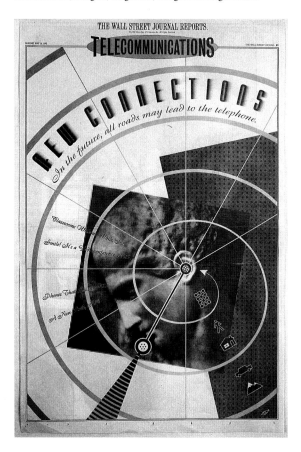

Bronze

The New York Times

Mirko Ilic, Art Director & Designer; Corinne Myller, Designer; Ruth Marten, Illustrator

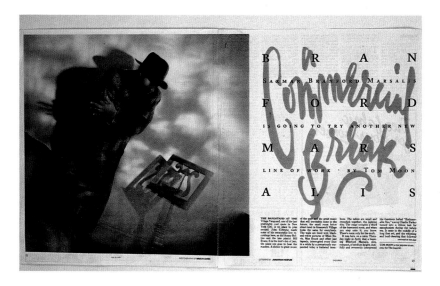

Award of Excellence

The Philadelphia Inquirer Magazine

Bert Fox, Art Director; Jessica Helfand, Designer, Design Director; Bruce Caines, Photographer; Jonathan Hoefler, Lettering; Bert Fox, Photo Editor

Award of Excellence

Detroit Free Press

Keith Webb, Designer

Award of Excellence

Diario 16

Madrid, Spain

Carlos Perez Diaz, Art Director & Designer; Montserrat Ortiz, Designer

BEFORE

Award of Excellence

El Nuevo Herald

Miami, FL

Nuri Ducassi, Art Director; Jose Pacheco, Designer

BEFORE

Award of Excellence

El Nuevo Herald

Miami, FL

Nuri Ducassi, Art Director; Jose Pacheco, Designer

BEFORE

AFTER

AFTER

AFTER

Award of Excellence
San Jose Mercury News

Sam Hundley, Features Design Director; Bryan Monroe, Design Director; Albert Poon, Designer; Doug Griswold, Artist; Sydney Fischer, Artist; Ed Clendaniel, Section Editor; Mike Jenner, Design Consultant; Bill Marr, Design Consultant; David Griffin, Design Consultant

BEFORE

Award of Excellence (also for page design)
Syracuse Newspapers

Syracuse, NY

Michael A. Braia, Staff Artist; Geoffrey Stickel, Art Director

BEFORE

Bronze
Nashville Banner

Nashville, TN

Jef Capaldi, Designer; Lucas Hendrickson, Graphics Editor

BEFORE

AFTER

AFTER

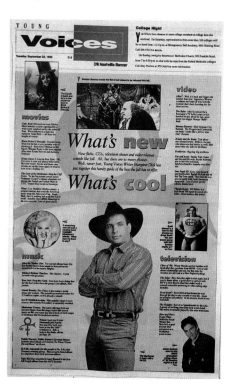

AFTER

Award of Excellence
The Charlotte Observer
Charlotte, NC
Sarah Blaydon, Designer; John Bordsen, Section Editor; Steve Snow, Section Editor

AFTER

Award of Excellence
The Charlotte Observer
Charlotte, NC
Jack Russell, Designer; Sarah Franquet, Designer; Sandy Hill, Section Editor

BEFORE

Award of Excellence
The Post-Standard
Syracuse, NY
Susan Santola, Art Director

AFTER

AFTER

AFTER

AFTER

NEW

Award of Excellence
The San Diego Union-Tribune
Ed Benguiat, Type Designer/Consultant

OLD

Award of Excellence
La Vanguardia
Barcelona, Spain
Carlos Perez de Rozas, Art Director; Rosa Mundet, Assistant
Art Director; Antoni Cases, Art Director; Narcis Bartra,
Graphics Artist

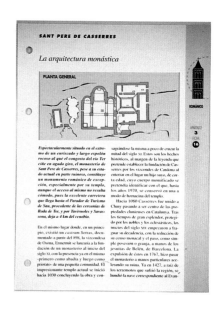

Award of Excellence
Richmond Times-Dispatch
Richmond, VA
John T. Ailor, Associate Graphics Director

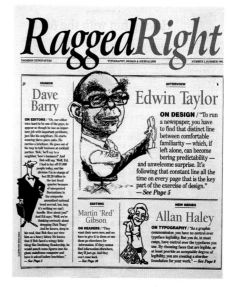

Award of Excellence
Ragged Right
Toronto, Canada
Tony Sutton, Editor & Designer; Brian Gable, Illustrator;
David Anderson, Illustrator; Alex Groen, Illustrator;
Bernard Bennell, Illustrator

Bronze & JSR
The New York Times
Tom Bodkin, Designer & Art Director; Sam Reep,
Designer; Ken McFarlin, Designer; Margaret O'Connor,
Designer; Paul Jean, Designer

Judges' Bios

Biografias Jueces

Maggie Balough has been editor of the *Austin American-Statesman* since 1988. She has worked on newspapers in Indiana, Florida and Illinois. She is a member of the Society of Professional Journalists, the American Society of Newspaper Editors and past president of SND. She was a SND contest judge for the 8th Edition (1986-87). She also has been an instructor in journalism at Northwestern University and the University of Texas at Austin.

Maggie Balough ha sido redactora del Austin American-Statesman desde 1988. Ha trabajado en periódicos en Indiana, Florida e Illinois. Es miembro de la Sociedad de Periodistas Profesionales, de la Sociedad Americana de Redactores de Periódicos y ha sido presidente de la SND. Fue juez de la 8ava Edición del concurso de la SND (1986-87). También ha enseñado periodismo en la Universidad Northwestern y en la Universidad de Texas en Austin.

George Berke is design director for *The Times-Picayune,* where he has worked since 1979. He has been art director of *New Orleans Magazine* and worked as designer and publisher of fine-art posters. He redesigned *The Times-Picayune* in 1984 and is currently redesigning it to incorporate the newest advances in color printing and digital technology.

George Berke es el director de diseño de The Times-Picayune, donde ha trabajado desde 1979. Ha sido director de arte del New Orleans Magazine y trabajó como diseñador y editor de pósters de bellas artes. Rediseñó The Times-Picayune en 1984 y actualmente lo está rediseñando para incorporar los últimos adelantos en impresión en color y tecnología digital.

Dierck Casselman, assistant managing editor for graphics and design at *The Detroit News,* chaired SND's 10th Edition judging. He worked as a reporter, copy editor, assistant city editor, feature editor and graphics editor at newspapers in Kansas and upstate New York before joining *The News* in 1987. He redesigned *The News* in 1990. He was on leave during spring 1993 to teach at the University of Nevada at Reno.

Dierck Casserman, asistente de redacción para gráficas y diseño de The Detroit News, presidió las deliberaciones de la 10a Edición de la SND. Trabajó como cronista, corrector, redactor asistente de ciudad, redactor de notas y editor de grafismo en periódicos de Kansas y del estado de Nueva York antes de unirse a The News en 1987. En 1990 rediseñó The Detroit News. Durante la primavera de 1993 estuvo en excedencia para enseñar en la Universidad de Nevada - Reno.

Tom Dolphens has been design director at *The Kansas City Star* for three years. Previously he was art director and a staff illustrator of *The Star, The Kansas City Times* and *The Omaha World-Herald*. Dolphens teaches illustration at the Kansas City Art Institute and has won SND, Society of Illustrators, Communication Arts, PRINT and American Illustration Annual awards.

Tom Dolphens ha sido director de diseño en The Kansas City Star durante los últimos tres años. Anteriormente fue director de arte e ilustrador para The Star, The Kansas City Times y The Omaha World-Herald. Dolphens enseña ilustración en el Instituto de Arte de Kansas City y ha ganado premios de la SND, la Sociedad de Ilustradores, de Artes de la Comunicación, de PRINT, y del certámen Anual de Ilustradores Americanos.

Mike Gordon is assistant managing editor of *The Atlanta Journal-Constitution.* He directs Sunday editions and is helping install a Mac-based pagination system. From 1989 to 1992 he redesigned the paper and ran its art department. He previously worked at the *Los Angeles Herald Examiner* and Riverside (CA) *Press-Enterprise* as a reporter, copy editor, news editor, editorial writer and graphics editor.

Mike Gordon es asistente de redacción de The Atlanta Journal Constitution. Dirige las ediciones de los domingos y está ayudando a instalar un sistema de paginación basado en el sistema MacIntosh. De 1989 a 1992 rediseñó el periódico y dirigió su departamento de arte. Anteriormente trabajó en el Los Angeles Herald Examiner y en Riverside, California, para el Press-Enterprise como cronista, corrector, redactor de noticias, escritor de editoriales y editor de grafismo.

Alan Jacobson, a newspaper design consultant, has redesigned more than a dozen newspapers. His work has been represented in annuals published by SND in each of the past 13 years. In 1991 the Society honored him with a Judges' Special Recognition for the overall design of five different newspapers. Prior to launching his own business, he was design director for Landmark Communications and *The Virginian-Pilot.*

Alan Jacobson, asesor de diseño de periódicos, ha rediseñado más de una docena de periódicos. Su trabajo ha sido representado en libros anuales publicados por la SND en cada uno de los últimos 13 años. En 1991 la Sociedad lo honró con el premio de Reconocimiento Especial de los Jueces por el diseño global de cinco periódicos diferentes. Antes de comenzar su propio negocio, fue director de diseño para Landmark Communications y para The Virginian-Pilot.

Alex Leary is an editorial artist at the *Saint Paul Pioneer Press,* where she has been for 10 years. She has been a "guest artist" at the Washington Bureau of Knight-Ridder-Tribune Graphics and was an "artist on loan" at *The Miami Herald* during its recovery from Hurricane Andrew.

Alex Leary es artista editorial en el Saint Paul Pioneer Press, donde ha estado desde hace 10 años. Ha sido "artista invitada" en la oficina de Knight-Ridder-Tribune Graphics en Washington y trabajó como "artista en préstamo" en The Miami Herald durante su recuperación del Huracán Adrew.

Elizabeth Mangelsdorf returned to the *San Francisco Examiner* in June 1993 as a staff photographer after taking a leave to teach photojournalism full-time at San Francisco State University. From 1990 to 1991 she was picture editor for *Image Magazine* of the *San Francisco Examiner.* She has been a free-lance photographer since 1984.

Elizabeth Mangelsdorf volvió al San Francisco Examiner en junio de 1993, como fotógrafa después de un período de excedencia para enseñar fotografía periodística a tiempo completo en la Universidad del Estado en San Francisco. Desde 1990 hasta 1991 fue editora de fotografía para la revista Image Magazine del San Francisco Examiner. Ha trabajado como fotógrafa free-lance desde 1984.

Ricardo Martinez is chief artist of *El Mundo,* Madrid, Spain. He has held graphics and design positions at *The Miami News* and was an artist for the Miami-based advertising agency Dominguez and Co. Martinez is an accomplished political cartoonist and comic strip author and has published two books.

Ricardo Martínez es artista en jefe de El Mundo, en Madrid, España. Ha ocupado puestos de gráficas y diseño en The Miami News y trabajó como artista para la agencia de publicidad Dominguez & Co., de Miami. Martínez es un caricaturista político y autor de tiras cómicas consumado, y ha publicado dos libros.

Scott Minister is art director and a designer for *The Columbus Dispatch* where he has been since 1985. He supervises a staff of graphic artists which produce daily feature section fronts, special sections, informational graphics and illustrations. *The Dispatch* has won numerous awards for graphic design and printing reproduction during the past few years.

Scott Minister es director de arte y diseñador para The Columbus Dispatch, donde trabaja desde 1985. Supervisa un plantel de artistas gráficos que producen portadas de crónicas, secciones especiales, gráficas informativas e ilustraciones diariamente. Durante los últimos años The Dispatch ha ganado varios premios por diseño gráfico e impresión y reproducción.

Karen Mitchell is deputy photography director at the *Des Moines Register* where she began following college. She returned to the *Register* in 1990 after spending six years at Gannett Rochester Newspapers as a staff photographer. She is currently involved in many of the *Register's* diversity organizations.

Karen Mitchell es vice-directora de fotografía en The Des Moines Register, donde comenzó a trabajar al salir de la universidad. Volvió al Register después de pasar seis años en Gannett Rochester Newspapers como integrante del plantel de fotógrafos. Actualmente está involucrada en varias de las diversas organizaciones del Register's.

S. Griffin (Griff) Singer has been active in journalism for more than 40 years, working in virtually all areas related to newspapering – printer, reporter, editor, educator and consultant. He is teaching full-time at the University of Texas at Austin. He also is a consultant to *The Houston Chronicle,* critiquing that publication's layout and design and writing through an electronic publication, *Singer's Zingers.*

S.Griffin (Griff) Singer ha estado trabajando en periodismo durante más de 40 años, prácticamente en todas las áreas relacionadas con los periódicos como impresor, cronista, redactor, educador y consultor. Enseña en la Universidad de Texas en Austin a tiempo completo. También es asesor de The Houston Chronicle, haciendo críticas de la diagramación y diseño de la publicación y escribiendo a través de una publicación electrónica, Singer's Zingers.

Nancy Smith has been the art director of *Ms.* magazine since 1991. Before joining *Ms.,* she was an art director for *The Washington Post,* designing the weekly Food and Outlook sections. Her newspaper portfolio won a Gold Award from SND in 1989.

Nancy Smith es directora de la revista Ms. desde 1991. Antes de unirse a Ms., fue directora de arte para The Washington Post, diseñando las secciones semanales de Gastronomía y Recreo. Su libro de presentación de sus trabajos en periódicos le valió un premio de Oro de SND en 1989.

Lynn Staley was named assistant managing editor/design for *The Boston Globe* in September 1989. Staley, who had been editorial design director at *The Globe* since 1987, redesigned the paper in 1989. She joined *The Globe* in 1980 and has overseen daily design issues and special projects. She was a SND contest judge for the 6th Edition (1984-85).

Lynn Staley fue nombrada asistente de redacción/diseño para The Boston Globe en septiembre de 1989. Staley, que había sido directora de diseño editorial en The Globe desde 1987, rediseñó el diario en 1989. Se unió a The Globe en 1980 y ha supervisado asuntos de diseño diario y proyectos especiales. Fue juez de concurso de la SND para la 6a Edición.

Nancy Tobin, SND's 1993 president, is president of Tobin Paperworks, a Buffalo, NY editorial/redesign consulting firm. She has been university publications director for SUNY-Buffalo, *Asbury Park Press* design director, *Buffalo News* graphics editor and *Buffalo Courier Express* art director. She has taught at Syracuse University's Newhouse School of Public Communications.

Nancy Tobin, presidente de la SND en 1993, es presidente de Tobin Paperworks, una empresa asesora de rediseño editorial de Buffalo, Nueva York. Ha sido directora de publicaciones para la universidad SUNY-Buffalo, directora de diseño del Asbury Park Press, directora gráfica de Buffalo News y directora de arte del Buffalo Courier Express. Ha enseñado en la Escuela Newhouse de la Universidad de Syracuse.

Gwendolyn Wong has spent 14 years creating page designs, logos, illustrations, constructions and images, most prominently for *The Boston Globe* and the *Orange County Register,* where she presently works. She has received awards from SND, Desi, New York Art Directors Club, Art Directors Club of Boston, Society of Illustrators and Three-Dimensional Illustrators competition.

Gwendolyn Wong ha pasado 14 años creando diseños de páginas, logotipos, ilustraciones, construcciones e imágenes, más prominentemente para The Boston Globe y The Orange County Register, donde trabaja actualmente. También ha recibido premios de la SND, de Desi, del Club de Directores de Arte de Nueva York, del Boston, de la Sociedad de Ilustradores y del certamen de Ilustradores Tridimensionales.

CREDITS: Special thanks to: G.W. Babb, Sam Babbage, Michael Braia, Renee Byer, Ray Chattman, Patty Coyle, Jef Capaldi, Travis Caperton, Paula Christian, Steve Dorsey, Nicolas Eyle, Julio Fernandez, Kent Fischer, Kelly Frankeny, Rosanna Grassi, Shauna Gellerman, Randy Grimshaw, Scott Goldman, Lora Gordon, Peter Harris, Michele Helm, Barbara Hines, Dave Horn, Mike Jantze, Jim Jennings, Paul Kalomiris, Samuel Kennedy, Joseph Kissel, Maria Lesch, Jonathan Levit, David Lindquist, Juan Lopez, Doug Maag, Kim Michalski, Michael Morgenthal, Pat O'Maley, Rob Owen, James Paschal, Dale Peskin, David Rubin, Joan Ruggaber, Bob Shields, Randy Stano, Barbara States, Shamus Walker.

INDEX

By Publication